FEDERAL RULES OF BANKRUPTCY PROCEDURE
2018 Edition

Updated through January 1, 2018

Michigan Legal Publishing Ltd.
QUICK DESK REFERENCE SERIES™

© 2015-2018 Michigan Legal Publishing Ltd.
Grand Rapids, Michigan

Academic and bulk discounts available at
www.michlp.com

WE WELCOME YOUR FEEDBACK: info@michlp.com

ISBN-13: 978-1-64002-024-5
ISBN-10: 1-64002-024-1

Table of Contents

Federal Rules of Bankruptcy Procedure

4

Rule 1001. Scope of Rules and Forms; Short Title

The Bankruptcy Rules and Forms govern procedure in cases under Title 11 of the United States Code. The rules shall be cited as the Federal Rules of Bankruptcy Procedure and the forms as the Official Bankruptcy Forms. These rules shall be construed, administered, and employed by the court and the parties to secure the just, speedy, and inexpensive determination of every case and proceeding.

Part I. Commencement of case: proceedings relating to petition and order for relief

Rule 1002. Commencement of Case

(a) **Petition**. A petition commencing a case under the Code shall be filed with the clerk.
(b) **Transmission to United States Trustee**. The clerk shall forthwith transmit to the United States trustee a copy of the petition filed pursuant to subdivision (a) of this rule.

Rule 1003. Involuntary Petition

(a) **Transferor or Transferee of Claim**. A transferor or transferee of a claim shall annex to the original and each copy of the petition a copy of all documents evidencing the transfer, whether transferred unconditionally, for security, or otherwise, and a signed statement that the claim was not transferred for the purpose of commencing the case and setting forth the consideration for and terms of the transfer. An entity that has transferred or acquired a claim for the purpose of commencing a case for liquidation under chapter 7 or for reorganization under chapter 11 shall not be a qualified petitioner.
(b) **Joinder of Petitioners After Filing**. If the answer to an involuntary petition filed by fewer than three creditors avers the existence of 12 or more creditors, the debtor shall file with the answer a list of all creditors with their addresses, a brief statement of the nature of their claims, and the amounts thereof. If it appears that there are 12 or more creditors as provided in § 303(b) of the Code, the court shall afford a reasonable opportunity for other creditors to join in the petition before a hearing is held thereon.

Rule 1004. Involuntary Petition Against a Partnership

After filing of an involuntary petition under § 303(b)(3) of the Code, (1) the petitioning partners or other petitioners shall promptly send to or serve on each general partner who is not a petitioner a copy of the petition; and (2) the clerk shall promptly issue a summons for service on each general partner who is not a petitioner. Rule 1010 applies to the form and service of the summons.

Rule 1004.1. Petition for an Infant or Incompetent Person

If an infant or incompetent person has a representative, including a general guardian, committee, conservator, or similar fiduciary, the representative may file a voluntary petition on behalf of the infant or incompetent person. An infant or incompetent person who does not have a duly appointed representative may file a voluntary petition by next friend or guardian ad litem. The court shall appoint a guardian ad litem for an infant or incompetent person who is a debtor and is not otherwise represented or shall make any other order to protect the infant or incompetent debtor.

Rule 1004.2. Petition in Chapter 15 Cases

(a) **Designating Center of Main Interests**. A petition for recognition of a foreign proceeding under chapter 15 of the Code shall state the country where the debtor has its center of main interests. The petition shall also identify each country in which a foreign proceeding by, regarding, or against the debtor is pending.

(b) **Challenging Designation**. The United States trustee or a party in interest may file a motion for a determination that the debtor's center of main interests is other than as stated in the petition for recognition commencing the chapter 15 case. Unless the court orders otherwise, the motion shall be filed no later than seven days before the date set for the hearing on the petition. The motion shall be transmitted to the United States trustee and served on the debtor, all persons or bodies authorized to administer foreign proceedings of the debtor, all entities against whom provisional relief is being sought under § 1519 of the Code, all parties to litigation pending in the United States in which the debtor was a party as of the time the petition was filed, and such other entities as the court may direct.

Rule 1005. Caption of Petition

The caption of a petition commencing a case under the Code shall contain the name of the court, the title of the case, and the docket number. The title of the case shall include the following information about the debtor: name, employer identification number, last four digits of the social-security number or individual debtor's taxpayer-identification number, any other federal taxpayer-identification number, and all other names used within eight years before filing the petition. If the petition is not filed by the debtor, it shall include all names used by the debtor which are known to the petitioners.

Rule 1006. Filing Fee

(a) **General Requirement**. Every petition shall be accompanied by the filing fee except as provided in subdivisions (b) and (c) of this rule. For the purpose of this rule, "filing fee" means the filing fee prescribed by 28 U.S.C. § 1930(a)(1)-(a)(5) and any other fee prescribed by the Judicial

Conference of the United States under 28 U.S.C. § 1930(b) that is payable to the clerk upon the commencement of a case under the Code.

(b) **Payment of Filing Fee in Installments.**

(1) *Application to Pay Filing Fee in Installments.* A voluntary petition by an individual shall be accepted for filing, regardless of whether any portion of the filing fee is paid, if accompanied by the debtor's signed application, prepared as prescribed by the appropriate Official Form, stating that the debtor is unable to pay the filing fee except in installments.

(2) *Action on Application.* Prior to the meeting of creditors, the court may order the filing fee paid to the clerk or grant leave to pay in installments and fix the number, amount and dates of payment. The number of installments shall not exceed four, and the final installment shall be payable not later than 120 days after filing the petition. For cause shown, the court may extend the time of any installment, provided the last installment is paid not later than 180 days after filing the petition.

(3) *Postponement of Attorney's Fees.* All installments of the filing fee must be paid in full before the debtor or chapter 13 trustee may make further payments to an attorney or any other person who renders services to the debtor in connection with the case.

Rule 1007. Lists, Schedules, Statements, and Other Documents; Time Limits

(a) **Corporate Ownership Statement, List of Creditors and Equity Security Holders, and Other Lists.**

(1) *Voluntary Case.* In a voluntary case, the debtor shall file with the petition a list containing the name and address of each entity included or to be included on Schedules D, E/F, G, and H as prescribed by the Official Forms. If the debtor is a corporation, other than a governmental unit, the debtor shall file with the petition a corporate ownership statement containing the information described in Rule 7007.1. The debtor shall file a supplemental statement promptly upon any change in circumstances that renders the corporate ownership statement inaccurate.

(2) *Involuntary Case.* In an involuntary case, the debtor shall file, within seven days after entry of the order for relief, a list containing the name and address of each entity included or to be included on Schedules D, E/F, G, and H as prescribed by the Official Forms.

(3) *Equity Security Holders.* In a chapter 11 reorganization case, unless the court orders otherwise, the debtor shall file within 14 days after entry of the order for relief a list of the debtor's equity security holders of each class showing the number and kind of interests

registered in the name of each holder, and the last known address or place of business of each holder.

(4) *Chapter 15 Case.* In addition to the documents required under § 1515 of the Code, a foreign representative filing a petition for recognition under chapter 15 shall file with the petition: (A) a corporate ownership statement containing the information described in Rule 7007.1; and (B) unless the court orders otherwise, a list containing the names and addresses of all persons or bodies authorized to administer foreign proceedings of the debtor, all parties to litigation pending in the United States in which the debtor is a party at the time of the filing of the petition, and all entities against whom provisional relief is being sought under § 1519 of the Code.

(5) *Extension of Time.* Any extension of time for the filing of the lists required by this subdivision may be granted only on motion for cause shown and on notice to the United States trustee and to any trustee, committee elected under § 705 or appointed under § 1102 of the Code, or other party as the court may direct.

(b) **Schedules, Statements, and Other Documents Required.**

(1) Except in a chapter 9 municipality case, the debtor, unless the court orders otherwise, shall file the following schedules, statements, and other documents, prepared as prescribed by the appropriate Official Forms, if any:

(A) schedules of assets and liabilities;

(B) a schedule of current income and expenditures;

(C) a schedule of executory contracts and unexpired leases;

(D) a statement of financial affairs;

(E) copies of all payment advices or other evidence of payment, if any, received by the debtor from an employer within 60 days before the filing of the petition, with redaction of all but the last four digits of the debtor's social-security number or individual taxpayer-identification number; and

(F) a record of any interest that the debtor has in an account or program of the type specified in § 521(c) of the Code.

(2) An individual debtor in a chapter 7 case shall file a statement of intention as required by § 521(a) of the Code, prepared as prescribed by the appropriate Official Form. A copy of the statement of intention shall be served on the trustee and the creditors named in the statement on or before the filing of the statement.

(3) Unless the United States trustee has determined that the credit counseling requirement of § 109(h) does not apply in the district, an individual debtor must file a statement of compliance with the credit counseling requirement, prepared as prescribed by the appropriate Official Form which must include one of the following:

      (A) an attached certificate and debt repayment plan, if any, required by § 521(b);

      (B) a statement that the debtor has received the credit counseling briefing required by § 109(h)(1) but does not have the certificate required by § 521(b);

      (C) a certification under § 109(h)(3); or

      (D) a request for a determination by the court under § 109(h)(4).

  (4) Unless § 707(b)(2)(D) applies, an individual debtor in a chapter 7 case shall file a statement of current monthly income prepared as prescribed by the appropriate Official Form, and, if the current monthly income exceeds the median family income for the applicable state and household size, the information, including calculations, required by § 707(b), prepared as prescribed by the appropriate Official Form.

  (5) An individual debtor in a chapter 11 case shall file a statement of current monthly income, prepared as prescribed by the appropriate Official Form.

  (6) A debtor in a chapter 13 case shall file a statement of current monthly income, prepared as prescribed by the appropriate Official Form, and, if the current monthly income exceeds the median family income for the applicable state and household size, a calculation of disposable income made in accordance with § 1325(b)(3), prepared as prescribed by the appropriate Official Form.

  (7) Unless an approved provider of an instructional course concerning personal financial management has notified the court that a debtor has completed the course after filing the petition:

      (A) An individual debtor in a chapter 7 or chapter 13 case shall file a statement of completion of the course, prepared as prescribed by the appropriate Official Form; and

      (B) An individual debtor in a chapter 11 case shall file the statement if § 1141(d)(3) applies.

  (8) If an individual debtor in a chapter 11, 12, or 13 case has claimed an exemption under § 522(b)(3)(A) in property of the kind described in § 522(p)(1) with a value in excess of the amount set out in § 522(q)(1), the debtor shall file a statement as to whether there is any proceeding pending in which the debtor may be found guilty of a felony of a kind described in § 522(q)(1)(A) or found liable for a debt of the kind described in § 522(q)(1)(B).

(c) **Time Limits.** In a voluntary case, the schedules, statements, and other documents required by subdivision (b)(1), (4), (5), and (6) shall be filed with the petition or within 14 days thereafter, except as otherwise provided in subdivisions (d), (e), (f), and (h) of this rule. In an involuntary case, the schedules, statements, and other documents required by subdivision (b)(1) shall be filed by the debtor within 14 days after the entry of the order for relief.

(d) **List of 20 Largest Creditors in Chapter 9 Municipality Case or Chapter 11 Reorganization Case**. In addition to the list required by subdivision (a) of this rule, a debtor in a chapter 9 municipality case or a debtor in a voluntary chapter 11 reorganization case shall file with the petition a list containing the name, address and claim of the creditors that hold the 20 largest unsecured claims, excluding insiders, as prescribed by the appropriate Official Form. In an involuntary chapter 11 reorganization case, such list shall be filed by the debtor within 2 days after entry of the order for relief under § 303(h) of the Code.

(e) **List in Chapter 9 Municipality Cases**. The list required by subdivision (a) of this rule shall be filed by the debtor in a chapter 9 municipality case within such time as the court shall fix. If a proposed plan requires a revision of assessments so that the proportion of special assessments or special taxes to be assessed against some real property will be different from the proportion in effect at the date the petition is filed, the debtor shall also file a list showing the name and address of each known holder of title, legal or equitable, to real property adversely affected. On motion for cause shown, the court may modify the requirements of this subdivision and subdivision (a) of this rule.

(f) **Statement of Social Security Number**. An individual debtor shall submit a verified statement that sets out the debtor's social security number, or states that the debtor does not have a social security number. In a voluntary case, the debtor shall submit the statement with the petition. In an involuntary case, the debtor shall submit the statement within 14 days after the entry of the order for relief.

(g) **Partnership and Partners**. The general partners of a debtor partnership shall prepare and file the list required under subdivision (a), the schedules of the assets and liabilities, schedule of current income and expenditures, schedule of executory contracts and unexpired leases, and statement of financial affairs of the partnership. The court may order any general partner to file a statement of personal assets and liabilities within such time as the court may fix.

(h) **Interests Acquired or Arising After Petition**. If, as provided by § 541(a)(5) of the Code, the debtor acquires or becomes entitled to acquire any interest in property, the debtor shall within 14 days after the information comes to the debtor's knowledge or within such further time the court may allow, file a supplemental schedule in the chapter 7 liquidation case, chapter 11 reorganization case, chapter 12 family farmer's debt adjustment case, or chapter 13 individual debt adjustment case. If any of the property required to be reported under this subdivision is claimed by the debtor as exempt, the debtor shall claim the exemptions in the supplemental schedule. The duty to file a supplemental schedule in accordance with this subdivision continues notwithstanding the closing of the case, except that the schedule need not be filed in a chapter 11, chapter 12, or chapter 13 case with respect to property acquired after entry of the order confirming a chapter 11 plan or discharging the debtor in a chapter 12 or chapter 13 case.

(i) **Disclosure of List of Security Holders.** After notice and hearing and for cause shown, the court may direct an entity other than the debtor or trustee to disclose any list of security holders of the debtor in its possession or under its control, indicating the name, address and security held by any of them. The entity possessing this list may be required either to produce the list or a true copy thereof, or permit inspection or copying, or otherwise disclose the information contained on the list.

(j) **Impounding of Lists.** On motion of a party in interest and for cause shown the court may direct the impounding of the lists filed under this rule, and may refuse to permit inspection by any entity. The court may permit inspection or use of the lists, however, by any party in interest on terms prescribed by the court.

(k) **Preparation of List, Schedules, or Statements on Default of Debtor.** If a list, schedule, or statement, other than a statement of intention, is not prepared and filed as required by this rule, the court may order the trustee, a petitioning creditor, committee, or other party to prepare and file any of these papers within a time fixed by the court. The court may approve reimbursement of the cost incurred in complying with such an order as an administrative expense.

(l) **Transmission to United States Trustee.** The clerk shall forthwith transmit to the United States trustee a copy of every list, schedule, and statement filed pursuant to subdivision (a)(1), (a)(2), (b), (d), or (h) of this rule.

(m) **Infants and Incompetent Persons.** If the debtor knows that a person on the list of creditors or schedules is an infant or incompetent person, the debtor also shall include the name, address, and legal relationship of any person upon whom process would be served in an adversary proceeding against the infant or incompetent person in accordance with Rule 7004(b)(2).

Rule 1008. Verification of Petitions and Accompanying Papers

All petitions, lists, schedules, statements and amendments thereto shall be verified or contain an unsworn declaration as provided in 28 U.S.C. § 1746.

Rule 1009. Amendments of Voluntary Petitions, Lists, Schedules and Statements

(a) **General Right to Amend.** A voluntary petition, list, schedule, or statement may be amended by the debtor as a matter of course at any time before the case is closed. The debtor shall give notice of the amendment to the trustee and to any entity affected thereby. On motion of a party in interest, after notice and a hearing, the court may order any voluntary petition, list, schedule, or statement to be amended and the clerk shall give notice of the amendment to entities designated by the court.

(b) **Statement of Intention.** The statement of intention may be amended by the debtor at any time before the expiration of the period provided in § 521(a) of the Code. The debtor shall give notice of the amendment to the trustee and to any entity affected thereby.

(c) **Statement of Social Security Number.** If a debtor becomes aware that the statement of social security number submitted under Rule 1007(f) is incorrect, the debtor shall promptly submit an amended verified statement setting forth the correct social security number. The debtor shall give notice of the amendment to all of the entities required to be included on the list filed under Rule 1007(a)(1) or (a)(2).

(d) **Transmission to United States Trustee.** The clerk shall promptly transmit to the United States trustee a copy of every amendment filed or submitted under subdivision (a), (b), or (c) of this rule.

Rule 1010. Service of Involuntary Petition and Summons

(a) **Service of Involuntary Petition and Summons.** On the filing of an involuntary petition, the clerk shall forthwith issue a summons for service. When an involuntary petition is filed, service shall be made on the debtor. The summons shall be served with a copy of the petition in the manner provided for service of a summons and complaint by Rule 7004(a) or (b). If service cannot be so made, the court may order that the summons and petition be served by mailing copies to the party's last known address, and by at least one publication in a manner and form directed by the court. The summons and petition may be served on the party anywhere. Rule 7004(e) and Rule 4(*l*) F. R. Civ. P. apply when service is made or attempted under this rule.

(b) **Corporate Ownership Statement.** Each petitioner that is a corporation shall file with the involuntary petition a corporate ownership statement containing the information described in Rule 7007.1.

Rule 1011. Responsive Pleading or Motion in Involuntary Cases

(a) **Who May Contest Petition.** The debtor named in an involuntary petition may contest the petition. In the case of a petition against a partnership under Rule 1004, a nonpetitioning general partner, or a person who is alleged to be a general partner but denies the allegation, may contest the petition.

(b) **Defenses and Objections; When Presented.** Defenses and objections to the petition shall be presented in the manner prescribed byRule 12 F. R. Civ. P. and shall be filed and served within 21 days after service of the summons, except that if service is made by publication on a party or partner not residing or found within the state in which the court sits, the court shall prescribe the time for filing and serving the response.

(c) **Effect of Motion.** Service of a motion under Rule 12(b) F. R. Civ. P. shall extend the time for filing and serving a responsive pleading as permitted by Rule 12(a) F. R. Civ. P.

(d) **Claims Against Petitioners.** A claim against a petitioning creditor may not be asserted in the answer except for the purpose of defeating the petition.

(e) **Other Pleadings.** No other pleadings shall be permitted, except that the court may order a reply to an answer and prescribe the time for filing and service.

(f) **Corporate Ownership Statement.** If the entity responding to the involuntary petition is a corporation, the entity shall file with its first appearance, pleading, motion, response, or other request addressed to the court a corporate ownership statement containing the information described in Rule 7007.1.

Rule 1012. Responsive Pleading in Cross-Border Cases

(a) **Who May Contest Petition.** The debtor or any party in interest may contest a petition for recognition of a foreign proceeding.

(b) **Objections and Responses; When Presented.** Objections and other responses to the petition shall be presented no later than seven days before the date set for the hearing on the petition, unless the court prescribes some other time or manner for responses.

(c) **Corporate Ownership Statement.** If the entity responding to the petition is a corporation, then the entity shall file a corporate ownership statement containing the information described in Rule 7007.1 with its first appearance, pleading, motion, response, or other request addressed to the court.

Rule 1013. Hearing and Disposition of a Petition in an Involuntary Case

(a) **Contested Petition.** The court shall determine the issues of a contested petition at the earliest practicable time and forthwith enter an order for relief, dismiss the petition, or enter any other appropriate order.

(b) **Default.** If no pleading or other defense to a petition is filed within the time provided by Rule 1011, the court, on the next day, or as soon thereafter as practicable, shall enter an order for the relief requested in the petition.

(c) [Abrogated]

Rule 1014. Dismissal and Change of Venue

(a) **Dismissal and Transfer of Cases.**

  (1) *Cases Filed in Proper District.* If a petition is filed in the proper district, the court, on the timely motion of a party in interest or on its own motion, and after hearing on notice to the petitioners, the United States trustee, and other entities as directed by the court, may transfer the case to any other district if the court determines that the transfer is in the interest of justice or for the convenience of the parties.

  (2) *Cases Filed in Improper District.* If a petition is filed in an improper district, the court, on the timely motion of a party in interest or on its own motion, and after hearing on notice to the petitioners, the United States trustee, and other entities as directed by the court, may dismiss the case or transfer it to any other district if the court determines that transfer is in the interest of justice or for the convenience of the parties.

(b) **Procedure When Petitions Involving the Same Debtor or Related Debtors Are Filed in Different Courts**. If petitions commencing cases under the Code or seeking recognition under chapter 15 are filed in different districts by, regarding, or against (1) the same debtor, (2) a partnership and one or more of its general partners, (3) two or more general partners, or (4) a debtor and an affiliate, the court in the district in which the first-filed petition is pending may determine, in the interest of justice or for the convenience of the parties, the district or districts in which any of the cases should proceed. The court may so determine on motion and after a hearing, with notice to the following entities in the affected cases: the United States trustee, entities entitled to notice under Rule 2002(a), and other entities as the court directs. The court may order the parties to the later-filed cases not to proceed further until it makes the determination.

Rule 1015. Consolidation or Joint Administration of Cases Pending in Same Court

(a) **Cases Involving Same Debtor**. If two or more petitions by, regarding, or against the same debtor are pending in the same court, the court may order consolidation of the cases.

(b) **Cases Involving Two or More Related Debtors**. If a joint petition or two or more petitions are pending in the same court by or against (1) spouses, or (2) a partnership and one or more of its general partners, or (3) two or more general partners, or (4) a debtor and an affiliate, the court may order a joint administration of the estates. Prior to entering an order the court shall give consideration to protecting creditors of different estates against potential conflicts of interest. An order directing joint administration of individual cases of spouses shall, if one spouse has elected the exemptions under § 522(b)(2) of the Code and the other has elected the exemptions under § 522(b)(3), fix a reasonable time within which either may amend the election so that both shall have elected the same exemptions. The order shall notify the debtors that unless they elect the same exemptions within the time fixed by the court, they will be deemed to have elected the exemptions provided by § 522(b)(2).

(c) **Expediting and Protective Orders**. When an order for consolidation or joint administration of a joint case or two or more cases is entered pursuant to this rule, while protecting the rights of the parties under the Code, the court may enter orders as may tend to avoid unnecessary costs and delay.

Rule 1016. Death or Incompetency of Debtor

Death or incompetency of the debtor shall not abate a liquidation case under chapter 7 of the Code. In such event the estate shall be administered and the case concluded in the same manner, so far as possible, as though the death or incompetency had not occurred. If a reorganization, family farmer's debt adjustment, or individual's debt adjustment case is pending under chapter 11, chapter 12, or chapter 13, the case may be dismissed; or if further administration is possible and in the best interest of the parties, the case may proceed and be concluded in the same manner, so far as possible, as though the death or incompetency had not occurred.

Rule 1017. Dismissal or Conversion of Case; Suspension

(a) **Voluntary Dismissal; Dismissal for Want of Prosecution or Other Cause**. Except as provided in §§ 707(a)(3), 707(b), 1208(b), and 1307(b) of the Code, and in Rule 1017(b), (c), and (e), a case shall not be dismissed on motion of the petitioner, for want of prosecution or other cause, or by consent of the parties, before a hearing on notice as provided in Rule 2002. For the purpose of the notice, the debtor shall file a list of creditors with their addresses within the time fixed by the court unless the list was previously filed. If the debtor fails to file the list, the court may order the debtor or another entity to prepare and file it.

(b) **Dismissal for Failure to Pay Filing Fee**.
  (1) If any installment of the filing fee has not been paid, the court may, after a hearing on notice to the debtor and the trustee, dismiss the case.
  (2) If the case is dismissed or closed without full payment of the filing fee, the installments collected shall be distributed in the same manner and proportions as if the filing fee had been paid in full.

(c) **Dismissal of Voluntary Chapter 7 or Chapter 13 Case for Failure to Timely File List of Creditors, Schedules, and Statement of Financial Affairs**. The court may dismiss a voluntary chapter 7 or chapter 13 case

22   *Rule 1018. Contested Involuntary Petitions; Contested Petitions*
Commencing Chapter 15 Cases; Proceedings to Vacate Order for Relief;
Applicability of Rules in Part VII Governing Adversary Proceedings

under § 707(a)(3) or § 1307(c)(9) after a hearing on notice served by the United States trustee on the debtor, the trustee, and any other entities as the court directs.

(d) **Suspension**. The court shall not dismiss a case or suspend proceedings under § 305 before a hearing on notice as provided in Rule 2002(a).

(e) **Dismissal of an Individual Debtor's Chapter 7 Case, or Conversion to a Case Under Chapter 11 or 13, for Abuse**. The court may dismiss or, with the debtor's consent, convert an individual debtor's case for abuse under § 707(b) only on motion and after a hearing on notice to the debtor, the trustee, the United States trustee, and any other entity as the court directs.

   (1) Except as otherwise provided in § 704(b)(2), a motion to dismiss a case for abuse under § 707(b) or (c) may be filed only within 60 days after the first date set for the meeting of creditors under § 341(a), unless, on request filed before the time has expired, the court for cause extends the time for filing the motion to dismiss. The party filing the motion shall set forth in the motion all matters to be considered at the hearing. In addition, a motion to dismiss under § 707(b)(1) and (3) shall state with particularity the circumstances alleged to constitute abuse.

   (2) If the hearing is set on the court's own motion, notice of the hearing shall be served on the debtor no later than 60 days after the first date set for the meeting of creditors under § 341(a). The notice shall set forth all matters to be considered by the court at the hearing.

(f) **Procedure for Dismissal, Conversion, or Suspension**.

   (1) Rule 9014 governs a proceeding to dismiss or suspend a case, or to convert a case to another chapter, except under §§ 706(a), 1112(a), 1208(a) or (b), or 1307(a) or (b).

   (2) Conversion or dismissal under §§ 706(a), 1112(a), 1208(b), or 1307(b) shall be on motion filed and served as required by Rule 9013.

   (3) A chapter 12 or chapter 13 case shall be converted without court order when the debtor files a notice of conversion under §§ 1208(a) or 1307(a). The filing date of the notice becomes the date of the conversion order for the purposes of applying § 348(c) and Rule 1019. The clerk shall promptly transmit a copy of the notice to the United States trustee.

Rule 1018. Contested Involuntary Petitions; Contested Petitions Commencing Chapter 15 Cases; Proceedings to Vacate Order for Relief; Applicability of Rules in Part VII Governing Adversary Proceedings

Unless the court otherwise directs and except as otherwise prescribed in Part I of these rules, the following rules in Part VII apply to all proceedings contesting an involuntary petition or a chapter 15 petition for recognition, and to all proceedings to vacate an order for relief: Rules 7005, 7008-7010, 7015, 7016, 7024-7026, 7028-7037, 7052, 7054, 7056, and 7062. The court may direct that other rules in Part VII shall also apply. For the purposes of this rule a reference in the Part VII rules to adversary proceedings shall be read as a reference to proceedings contesting an involuntary petition or a chapter 15 petition for recognition, or proceedings to vacate an order for relief. Reference in the Federal Rules of Civil Procedure to the complaint shall be read as a reference to the petition.

Rule 1019. Conversion of a Chapter 11 Reorganization Case, Chapter 12 Family Farmer's Debt Adjustment Case, or Chapter 13 Individual's Debt Adjustment Case to a Chapter 7 Liquidation Case

When a chapter 11, chapter 12, or chapter 13 case has been converted or reconverted to a chapter 7 case:

(1) **Filing of Lists, Inventories, Schedules, Statements**.

(A) Lists, inventories, schedules, and statements of financial affairs theretofore filed shall be deemed to be filed in the chapter 7 case, unless the court directs otherwise. If they have not been previously filed, the debtor shall comply with Rule 1007 as if an order for relief had been entered on an involuntary petition on the date of the entry of the order directing that the case continue under chapter 7.

(B) If a statement of intention is required, it shall be filed within 30 days after entry of the order of conversion or before the first date set for the meeting of creditors, whichever is earlier. The court may grant an extension of time for cause only on written motion filed, or oral request made during a hearing, before the time has expired. Notice of an extension shall be given to the United States trustee and to any committee, trustee, or other party as the court may direct.

(2) **New Filing Periods**.

(A) A new time period for filing a motion under § 707(b) or (c), a claim, a complaint objecting to discharge, or a complaint to obtain a determination of dischargeability of any debt shall commence under Rules 1017, 3002, 4004, or 4007, but a new time period shall not commence if a chapter 7 case had been converted to a chapter 11, 12, or 13 case and thereafter reconverted to a chapter 7 case and the time for filing a motion under § 707(b) or (c), a claim, a complaint objecting to discharge, or a complaint to obtain a determination of the dischargeability of any debt, or any extension thereof, expired in the original chapter 7 case.

(B) A new time period for filing an objection to a claim of exemptions shall commence under Rule 4003(b) after conversion of a case to chapter 7 unless:

    (i) the case was converted to chapter 7 more than one year after the entry of the first order confirming a plan under chapter 11, 12, or 13; or

    (ii) the case was previously pending in chapter 7 and the time to object to a claimed exemption had expired in the original chapter 7 case.

(3) **Claims Filed Before Conversion.** All claims actually filed by a creditor before conversion of the case are deemed filed in the chapter 7 case.

(4) **Turnover of Records and Property.** After qualification of, or assumption of duties by the chapter 7 trustee, any debtor in possession or trustee previously acting in the chapter 11, 12, or 13 case shall, forthwith, unless otherwise ordered, turn over to the chapter 7 trustee all records and property of the estate in the possession or control of the debtor in possession or trustee.

(5) **Filing Final Report and Schedule of Postpetition Debts.**

(A) Conversion of Chapter 11 or Chapter 12 Case. Unless the court directs otherwise, if a chapter 11 or chapter 12 case is converted to chapter 7, the debtor in possession or, if the debtor is not a debtor in possession, the trustee serving at the time of conversion, shall:

    (i) not later than 14 days after conversion of the case, file a schedule of unpaid debts incurred after the filing of the petition and before conversion of the case, including the name and address of each holder of a claim; and

    (ii) not later than 30 days after conversion of the case, file and transmit to the United States trustee a final report and account;

(B) Conversion of Chapter 13 Case. Unless the court directs otherwise, if a chapter 13 case is converted to chapter 7,

    (i) the debtor, not later than 14 days after conversion of the case, shall file a schedule of unpaid debts incurred after the filing of the petition and before conversion of the case, including the name and address of each holder of a claim; and

    (ii) the trustee, not later than 30 days after conversion of the case, shall file and transmit to the United States trustee a final report and account;

(C) Conversion After Confirmation of a Plan. Unless the court orders otherwise, if a chapter 11, chapter 12, or chapter 13 case is converted to chapter 7 after confirmation of a plan, the debtor shall file:

        (i) a schedule of property not listed in the final report and account acquired after the filing of the petition but before conversion, except if the case is converted from chapter 13 to chapter 7 and § 348(f)(2) does not apply;

        (ii) a schedule of unpaid debts not listed in the final report and account incurred after confirmation but before the conversion; and

        (iii) a schedule of executory contracts and unexpired leases entered into or assumed after the filing of the petition but before conversion.

    (D) Transmission to United States Trustee. The clerk shall forthwith transmit to the United States trustee a copy of every schedule filed pursuant to Rule 1019(5).

  (6) **Postpetition Claims; Preconversion Administrative Expenses; Notice**. A request for payment of an administrative expense incurred before conversion of the case is timely filed under § 503(a) of the Code if it is filed before conversion or a time fixed by the court. If the request is filed by a governmental unit, it is timely if it is filed before conversion or within the later of a time fixed by the court or 180 days after the date of the conversion. A claim of a kind specified in § 348(d) may be filed in accordance with Rules 3001(a)-(d) and 3002. Upon the filing of the schedule of unpaid debts incurred after commencement of the case and before conversion, the clerk, or some other person as the court may direct, shall give notice to those entities listed on the schedule of the time for filing a request for payment of an administrative expense and, unless a notice of insufficient assets to pay a dividend is mailed in accordance with Rule 2002(e), the time for filing a claim of a kind specified in § 348(d).

  (7) [Abrogated]

Rule 1020. Small Business Chapter 11 Reorganization Case

(a) **Small Business Debtor Designation**. In a voluntary chapter 11 case, the debtor shall state in the petition whether the debtor is a small business debtor. In an involuntary chapter 11 case, the debtor shall file within 14 days after entry of the order for relief a statement as to whether the debtor is a small business debtor. Except as provided in subdivision (c), the status of the case as a small business case shall be in accordance with the debtor's statement under this subdivision, unless and until the court enters an order finding that the debtor's statement is incorrect.

(b) **Objecting to Designation**. Except as provided in subdivision (c), the United States trustee or a party in interest may file an objection to the debtor's statement under subdivision (a) no later than 30 days after the conclusion of the meeting of creditors held under § 341(a) of the Code, or within 30 days after any amendment to the statement, whichever is later.

(c) **Appointment of Committee of Unsecured Creditors**. If a committee of unsecured creditors has been appointed under § 1102(a)(1), the case shall proceed as a small business case only if, and from the time when, the court enters an order determining that the committee has not been sufficiently active and representative to provide effective oversight of the debtor and that the debtor satisfies all the other requirements for being a small business. A request for a determination under this subdivision may be filed by the United States trustee or a party in interest only within a reasonable time after the failure of the committee to be sufficiently active and representative. The debtor may file a request for a determination at any time as to whether the committee has been sufficiently active and representative.

(d) **Procedure for Objection or Determination**. Any objection or request for a determination under this rule shall be governed by Rule 9014 and served on: the debtor; the debtor's attorney; the United States trustee; the trustee; any committee appointed under § 1102 or its authorized agent, or, if no committee of unsecured creditors has been appointed under § 1102, the creditors included on the list filed under Rule 1007(d); and any other entity as the court directs.

Rule 1021. Health Care Business Case

(a) **Health Care Business Designation**. Unless the court orders otherwise, if a petition in a case under chapter 7, chapter 9, or chapter 11 states that the debtor is a health care business, the case shall proceed as a case in which the debtor is a health care business.

(b) **Motion**. The United States trustee or a party in interest may file a motion to determine whether the debtor is a health care business. The motion shall be transmitted to the United States trustee and served on: the debtor; the trustee; any committee elected under § 705 or appointed under § 1102 of the Code or its authorized agent, or, if the case is a chapter 9 municipality case or a chapter 11 reorganization case and no committee of unsecured creditors has been appointed under § 1102, the creditors included on the list filed under Rule 1007(d); and any other entity as the court directs. The motion shall be governed by Rule 9014.

Part II. Officers and administration; notices; meetings; examinations; elections; attorneys and accountants

Rule 2001. Appointment of Interim Trustee Before Order for Relief in a Chapter 7 Liquidation Case

(a) **Appointment.** At any time following the commencement of an involuntary liquidation case and before an order for relief, the court on written motion of a party in interest may order the appointment of an interim trustee under § 303(g) of the Code. The motion shall set forth the necessity for the appointment and may be granted only after hearing on notice to the debtor, the petitioning creditors, the United States trustee, and other parties in interest as the court may designate.

(b) **Bond of Movant.** An interim trustee may not be appointed under this rule unless the movant furnishes a bond in an amount approved by the court, conditioned to indemnify the debtor for costs, attorney's fee, expenses, and damages allowable under § 303(i) of the Code.

(c) **Order of Appointment.** The order directing the appointment of an interim trustee shall state the reason the appointment is necessary and shall specify the trustee's duties.

(d) **Turnover and Report.** Following qualification of the trustee selected under § 702 of the Code, the interim trustee, unless otherwise ordered, shall (1) forthwith deliver to the trustee all the records and property of the estate in possession or subject to control of the interim trustee and, (2) within 30 days thereafter file a final report and account.

Rule 2002. Notices to Creditors, Equity Security Holders, Administrators in Foreign Proceedings, Persons Against Whom Provisional Relief is Sought in Ancillary and Other Cross-Border Cases, United States, and United States Trustee

(a) **Twenty-One-Day Notices to Parties in Interest.** Except as provided in subdivisions (h), (i), (l), (p), and (q) of this rule, the clerk, or some other person as the court may direct, shall give the debtor, the trustee, all creditors and indenture trustees at least 21 days' notice by mail of:

    (1) the meeting of creditors under § 341 or § 1104(b) of the Code, which notice, unless the court orders otherwise, shall include the debtor's employer identification number, Social Security number, and any other federal taxpayer identification number;

    (2) a proposed use, sale, or lease of property of the estate other than in the ordinary course of business, unless the court for cause shown shortens the time or directs another method of giving notice;

    (3) the hearing on approval of a compromise or settlement of a controversy other than approval of an agreement pursuant to Rule

4001(d), unless the court for cause shown directs that notice not be sent;

(4) in a chapter 7 liquidation, a chapter 11 reorganization case, or a chapter 12 family farmer debt adjustment case, the hearing on the dismissal of the case or the conversion of the case to another chapter, unless the hearing is under § 707(a)(3) or § 707(b) or is on dismissal of the case for failure to pay the filing fee;

(5) the time fixed to accept or reject a proposed modification of a plan;

(6) a hearing on any entity's request for compensation or reimbursement of expenses if the request exceeds $1,000;

(7) the time fixed for filing proofs of claims pursuant to Rule 3003(c);

(8) the time fixed for filing objections and the hearing to consider confirmation of a chapter 12 plan; and

(9) the time fixed for filing objections to confirmation of a chapter 13 plan.

(b) **Twenty-Eight-Day Notices to Parties in Interest**. Except as provided in subdivision (l) of this rule, the clerk, or some other person as the court may direct, shall give the debtor, the trustee, all creditors and indenture trustees not less than 28 days notice by mail of the time fixed (1) for filing objections and the hearing to consider approval of a disclosure statement or, under § 1125(f), to make a final determination whether the plan provides adequate information so that a separate disclosure statement is not necessary; (2) for filing objections and the hearing to consider confirmation of a chapter 9 or chapter 11 plan; and (3) for the hearing to consider confirmation of a chapter 13 plan.

(c) **Content of Notice**.

(1) *Proposed Use, Sale, or Lease of Property*. Subject to Rule 6004, the notice of a proposed use, sale, or lease of property required by subdivision (a)(2) of this rule shall include the time and place of any public sale, the terms and conditions of any private sale and the time fixed for filing objections. The notice of a proposed use, sale, or lease of property, including real estate, is sufficient if it generally describes the property. The notice of a proposed sale or lease of personally identifiable information under § 363(b)(1) of the Code shall state whether the sale is consistent with any policy prohibiting the transfer of the information.

(2) *Notice of Hearing on Compensation*. The notice of a hearing on an application for compensation or reimbursement of expenses required by subdivision (a)(6) of this rule shall identify the applicant and the amounts requested.

(3) *Notice of Hearing on Confirmation When Plan Provides for an Injunction*. If a plan provides for an injunction against conduct not otherwise enjoined under the Code, the notice required under Rule 2002(b)(2) shall:

(A) include in conspicuous language (bold, italic, or underlined text) a statement that the plan proposes an injunction;

(B) describe briefly the nature of the injunction; and

(C) identify the entities that would be subject to the injunction.

(d) **Notice to Equity Security Holders.** In a chapter 11 reorganization case, unless otherwise ordered by the court, the clerk, or some other person as the court may direct, shall in the manner and form directed by the court give notice to all equity security holders of (1) the order for relief; (2) any meeting of equity security holders held pursuant to § 341 of the Code; (3) the hearing on the proposed sale of all or substantially all of the debtor's assets; (4) the hearing on the dismissal or conversion of a case to another chapter; (5) the time fixed for filing objections to and the hearing to consider approval of a disclosure statement; (6) the time fixed for filing objections to and the hearing to consider confirmation of a plan; and (7) the time fixed to accept or reject a proposed modification of a plan.

(e) **Notice of No Dividend.** In a chapter 7 liquidation case, if it appears from the schedules that there are no assets from which a dividend can be paid, the notice of the meeting of creditors may include a statement to that effect; that it is unnecessary to file claims; and that if sufficient assets become available for the payment of a dividend, further notice will be given for the filing of claims.

(f) **Other Notices.** Except as provided in subdivision (l) of this rule, the clerk, or some other person as the court may direct, shall give the debtor, all creditors, and indenture trustees notice by mail of:

(1) the order for relief;

(2) the dismissal or the conversion of the case to another chapter, or the suspension of proceedings under § 305;

(3) the time allowed for filing claims pursuant to Rule 3002;

(4) the time fixed for filing a complaint objecting to the debtor's discharge pursuant to § 727 of the Code as provided in Rule 4004;

(5) the time fixed for filing a complaint to determine the dischargeability of a debt pursuant to § 523 of the Code as provided in Rule 4007;

(6) the waiver, denial, or revocation of a discharge as provided in Rule 4006;

(7) entry of an order confirming a chapter 9, 11, or 12 plan;

(8) a summary of the trustee's final report in a chapter 7 case if the net proceeds realized exceed $1,500;

(9) a notice under Rule 5008 regarding the presumption of abuse;

(10) a statement under § 704(b)(1) as to whether the debtor's case would be presumed to be an abuse under § 707(b); and

(11) the time to request a delay in the entry of the discharge under §§ 1141(d)(5)(C), 1228(f), and 1328(h).

Notice of the time fixed for accepting or rejecting a plan pursuant to Rule 3017(c) shall be given in accordance with Rule 3017(d).

(g) **Addressing Notices.**

    (1) Notices required to be mailed under Rule 2002 to a creditor, indenture trustee, or equity security holder shall be addressed as such entity or an authorized agent has directed in its last request filed in the particular case. For the purposes of this subdivision –

        (A) a proof of claim filed by a creditor or indenture trustee that designates a mailing address constitutes a filed request to mail notices to that address, unless a notice of no dividend has been given under Rule 2002(e) and a later notice of possible dividend under Rule 3002(c)(5) has not been given; and

        (B) a proof of interest filed by an equity security holder that designates a mailing address constitutes a filed request to mail notices to that address.

    (2) Except as provided in § 342(f) of the Code, if a creditor or indenture trustee has not filed a request designating a mailing address under Rule 2002(g)(1) or Rule 5003(e), the notices shall be mailed to the address shown on the list of creditors or schedule of liabilities, whichever is filed later. If an equity security holder has not filed a request designating a mailing address under Rule 2002(g)(1) or Rule 5003(e), the notices shall be mailed to the address shown on the list of equity security holders.

    (3) If a list or schedule filed under Rule 1007 includes the name and address of a legal representative of an infant or incompetent person, and a person other than that representative files a request or proof of claim designating a name and mailing address that differs from the name and address of the representative included in the list or schedule, unless the court orders otherwise, notices under Rule 2002 shall be mailed to the representative included in the list or schedules and to the name and address designated in the request or proof of claim.

    (4) Notwithstanding Rule 2002(g)(1)-(3), an entity and a notice provider may agree that when the notice provider is directed by the court to give a notice, the notice provider shall give the notice to the entity in the manner agreed to and at the address or addresses the entity supplies to the notice provider. That address is conclusively presumed to be a proper address for the notice. The notice provider's failure to use the supplied address does not invalidate any notice that is otherwise effective under applicable law.

    (5) A creditor may treat a notice as not having been brought to the creditor's attention under § 342(g)(1) only if, prior to issuance of the notice, the creditor has filed a statement that designates the name and address of the person or organizational subdivision of the creditor responsible for receiving notices under the Code, and that describes

the procedures established by the creditor to cause such notices to be delivered to the designated person or subdivision.

(h) **Notices to Creditors Whose Claims Are Filed.** In a chapter 7 case, after 90 days following the first date set for the meeting of creditors under § 341 of the Code, the court may direct that all notices required by subdivision (a) of this rule be mailed only to the debtor, the trustee, all indenture trustees, creditors that hold claims for which proofs of claim have been filed, and creditors, if any, that are still permitted to file claims by reason of an extension granted pursuant to Rule 3002(c)(1) or (c)(2). In a case where notice of insufficient assets to pay a dividend has been given to creditors pursuant to subdivision (e) of this rule, after 90 days following the mailing of a notice of the time for filing claims pursuant to Rule 3002(c)(5), the court may direct that notices be mailed only to the entities specified in the preceding sentence.

(i) **Notices to Committees.** Copies of all notices required to be mailed pursuant to this rule shall be mailed to the committees elected under § 705 or appointed under § 1102 of the Code or to their authorized agents. Notwithstanding the foregoing subdivisions, the court may order that notices required by subdivision (a)(2), (3) and (6) of this rule be transmitted to the United States trustee and be mailed only to the committees elected under § 705 or appointed under § 1102 of the Code or to their authorized agents and to the creditors and equity security holders who serve on the trustee or debtor in possession and file a request that all notices be mailed to them. A committee appointed under § 1114 shall receive copies of all notices required by subdivisions (a)(1), (a)(5), (b), (f)(2), and (f)(7), and such other notices as the court may direct.

(j) **Notices to the United States.** Copies of notices required to be mailed to all creditors under this rule shall be mailed (1) in a chapter 11 reorganization case, to the Securities and Exchange Commission at any place the Commission designates, if the Commission has filed either a notice of appearance in the case or a written request to receive notices; (2) in a commodity broker case, to the Commodity Futures Trading Commission at Washington, D.C.; (3) in a chapter 11 case to the Internal Revenue Service at its address set out in the register maintained under Rule 5003(e) for the district in which the case is pending; (4) if the papers in the case disclose a debt to the United States other than for taxes, to the United States attorney for the district in which the case is pending and to the department, agency, or instrumentality of the United States through which the debtor became indebted; or (5) if the filed papers disclose a stock interest of the United States, to the Secretary of the Treasury at Washington, D.C.

(k) **Notices to United States Trustee.** Unless the case is a chapter 9 municipality case or unless the United States trustee requests otherwise, the clerk, or some other person as the court may direct, shall transmit to the United States trustee notice of the matters described in subdivisions (a)(2), (a)(3), (a)(4), (a)(8), (b), (f)(1), (f)(2), (f)(4), (f)(6), (f)(7), (f)(8), and (q) of this rule and notice of hearings on all applications for compensation or reimbursement of expenses. Notices to the United States trustee shall be transmitted within the time prescribed in subdivision (a) or (b) of this rule. The United States trustee shall also receive notice of any other matter if such notice is requested by the United States trustee or ordered by the court. Nothing in these rules requires the clerk or any other person to transmit to the United States trustee any notice, schedule, report, application or other document in a case under the Securities Investor Protection Act,15 U.S.C. §§ 78aaa et seq.

(l)   **Notice by Publication.** The court may order notice by publication if it finds that notice by mail is impracticable or that it is desirable to supplement the notice.

(m)   **Orders Designating Matter of Notices.** The court may from time to time enter orders designating the matters in respect to which, the entity to whom, and the form and manner in which notices shall be sent except as otherwise provided by these rules.

(n)   **Caption.** The caption of every notice given under this rule shall comply with Rule 1005. The caption of every notice required to be given by the debtor to a creditor shall include the information required to be in the notice by § 342(c) of the Code.

(o)   **Notice of Order for Relief in Consumer Case.** In a voluntary case commenced by an individual debtor whose debts are primarily consumer debts, the clerk or some other person as the court may direct shall give the trustee and all creditors notice by mail of the order for relief within 21 days from the date thereof.

(p)   **Notice to a Creditor with a Foreign Address.**

    (1) If, at the request of the United States trustee or a party in interest, or on its own initiative, the court finds that a notice mailed within the time prescribed by these rules would not be sufficient to give a creditor with a foreign address to which notices under these rules are mailed reasonable notice under the circumstances, the court may order that the notice be supplemented with notice by other means or that the time prescribed for the notice by mail be enlarged.

    (2) Unless the court for cause orders otherwise, a creditor with a foreign address to which notices under this rule are mailed shall be given at least 30 days' notice of the time fixed for filing a proof of claim under Rule 3002(c) or Rule 3003(c).

    (3) Unless the court for cause orders otherwise, the mailing address of a creditor with a foreign address shall be determined under Rule 2002(g).

(q)   **Notice of Petition for Recognition of Foreign Proceeding and of Court's Intention to Communicate with Foreign Courts and Foreign Representatives.**

(1) *Notice of Petition for Recognition.* After the filing of a petition for recognition of a foreign proceeding, the court shall promptly schedule and hold a hearing on the petition. The clerk, or some other person as the court may direct, shall forthwith give the debtor, all persons or bodies authorized to administer foreign proceedings of the debtor, all entities against whom provisional relief is being sought under § 1519 of the Code, all parties to litigation pending in the United States in which the debtor is a party at the time of the filing of the petition, and such other entities as the court may direct, at least 21 days' notice by mail of the hearing. The notice shall state whether the petition seeks recognition as a foreign main proceeding or foreign nonmain proceeding and shall include the petition and any other document the court may require. If the court consolidates the hearing on the petition with the hearing on a request for provisional relief, the court may set a shorter notice period, with notice to the entities listed in this subdivision.

(2) *Notice of Court's Intention to Communicate with Foreign Courts and Foreign Representatives.* The clerk, or some other person as the court may direct, shall give the debtor, all persons or bodies authorized to administer foreign proceedings of the debtor, all entities against whom provisional relief is being sought under § 1519 of the Code, all parties to litigation pending in the United States in which the debtor is a party at the time of the filing of the petition, and such other entities as the court may direct, notice by mail of the court's intention to communicate with a foreign court or foreign representative.

Rule 2003. Meeting of Creditors or Equity Security Holders

(a) **Date and Place.** Except as otherwise provided in § 341(e) of the Code, in a chapter 7 liquidation or a chapter 11 reorganization case, the United States trustee shall call a meeting of creditors to be held no fewer than 21 and no more than 40 days after the order for relief. In a chapter 12 family farmer debt adjustment case, the United States trustee shall call a meeting of creditors to be held no fewer than 21 and no more than 35 days after the order for relief. In a chapter 13 individual's debt adjustment case, the United States trustee shall call a meeting of creditors to be held no fewer than 21 and no more than 50 days after the order for relief. If there is an appeal from or a motion to vacate the order for relief, or if there is a motion to dismiss the case, the United States trustee may set a later date for the meeting. The meeting may be held at a regular place for holding court or at any other place designated by the United States trustee within the district convenient for the parties in interest. If the United States trustee designates a place for the meeting which is not regularly staffed by the United States trustee or an assistant who may preside at the meeting, the meeting may be held not more than 60 days after the order for relief.

(b) **Order of Meeting.**

(1) *Meeting of Creditors.* The United States trustee shall preside at the meeting of creditors. The business of the meeting shall include the examination of the debtor under oath and, in a chapter 7 liquidation case, may include the election of a creditors' committee and, if the case is not under subchapter V of chapter 7, the election of a trustee. The presiding officer shall have the authority to administer oaths.

(2) *Meeting of Equity Security Holders.* If the United States trustee convenes a meeting of equity security holders pursuant to § 341(b) of the Code, the United States trustee shall fix a date for the meeting and shall preside.

(3) *Right To Vote.* In a chapter 7 liquidation case, a creditor is entitled to vote at a meeting if, at or before the meeting, the creditor has filed a proof of claim or a writing setting forth facts evidencing a right to vote pursuant to § 702(a) of the Code unless objection is made to the claim or the proof of claim is insufficient on its face. A creditor of a partnership may file a proof of claim or writing evidencing a right to vote for the trustee for the estate of the general partner notwithstanding that a trustee for the estate of the partnership has previously qualified. In the event of an objection to the amount or allowability of a claim for the purpose of voting, unless the court orders otherwise, the United States trustee shall tabulate the votes for each alternative presented by the dispute and, if resolution of such dispute is necessary to determine the result of the election, the tabulations for each alternative shall be reported to the court.

(c) **Record of Meeting.** Any examination under oath at the meeting of creditors held pursuant to § 341(a) of the Code shall be recorded verbatim by the United States trustee using electronic sound recording equipment or other means of recording, and such record shall be preserved by the United States trustee and available for public access until two years after the conclusion of the meeting of creditors. Upon request of any entity, the United States trustee shall certify and provide a copy or transcript of such recording at the entity's expense.

(d) **Report of Election and Resolution of Disputes in a Chapter 7 Case.**

(1) *Report of Undisputed Election.* In a chapter 7 case, if the election of a trustee or a member of a creditors' committee is not disputed, the United States trustee shall promptly file a report of the election, including the name and address of the person or entity elected and a statement that the election is undisputed.

(2) *Disputed Election.* If the election is disputed, the United States trustee shall promptly file a report stating that the election is disputed, informing the court of the nature of the dispute, and listing the name and address of any candidate elected under any alternative presented by the dispute. No later than the date on which the report is filed, the United States trustee shall mail a copy of the report to any party in interest that has made a request to receive a copy of the report. Pending disposition by the court of a disputed election for trustee, the interim trustee shall continue in office. Unless a motion for the

resolution of the dispute is filed no later than 14 days after the United States trustee files a report of a disputed election for trustee, the interim trustee shall serve as trustee in the case.

(e) **Adjournment.** The meeting may be adjourned from time to time by announcement at the meeting of the adjourned date and time. The presiding official shall promptly file a statement specifying the date and time to which the meeting is adjourned.

(f) **Special Meetings.** The United States trustee may call a special meeting of creditors on request of a party in interest or on the United States trustee's own initiative.

(g) **Final Meeting.** If the United States trustee calls a final meeting of creditors in a case in which the net proceeds realized exceed $1,500, the clerk shall mail a summary of the trustee's final account to the creditors with a notice of the meeting, together with a statement of the amount of the claims allowed. The trustee shall attend the final meeting and shall, if requested, report on the administration of the estate.

Rule 2004. Examination

(a) **Examination on Motion.** On motion of any party in interest, the court may order the examination of any entity.

(b) **Scope of Examination.** The examination of an entity under this rule or of the debtor under § 343 of the Code may relate only to the acts, conduct, or property or to the liabilities and financial condition of the debtor, or to any matter which may affect the administration of the debtor's estate, or to the debtor's right to a discharge. In a family farmer's debt adjustment case under chapter 12, an individual's debt adjustment case under chapter 13, or a reorganization case under chapter 11 of the Code, other than for the reorganization of a railroad, the examination may also relate to the operation of any business and the desirability of its continuance, the source of any money or property acquired or to be acquired by the debtor for purposes of consummating a plan and the consideration given or offered therefor, and any other matter relevant to the case or to the formulation of a plan.

(c) **Compelling Attendance and Production of Documents.** The attendance of an entity for examination and for the production of documents, whether the examination is to be conducted within or without the district in which the case is pending, may be compelled as provided in Rule 9016 for the attendance of a witness at a hearing or trial. As an officer of the court, an attorney may issue and sign a subpoena on behalf of the court for the district in which the examination is to be held if the attorney is admitted to practice in that court or in the court in which the case is pending.

(d) **Time and Place of Examination of Debtor.** The court may for cause shown and on terms as it may impose order the debtor to be examined under this rule at any time or place it designates, whether within or without the district wherein the case is pending.

(e) **Mileage.** An entity other than a debtor shall not be required to attend as a witness unless lawful mileage and witness fee for one day's attendance shall be first tendered. If the debtor resides more than 100 miles from the place of examination when required to appear for an examination under this rule, the mileage allowed by law to a witness shall be tendered for any distance more than 100 miles from the debtor's residence at the date of the filing of the first petition commencing a case under the Code or the residence at the time the debtor is required to appear for the examination, whichever is the lesser.

Rule 2005. Apprehension and Removal of Debtor to Compel Attendance for Examination

(a) **Order to Compel Attendance for Examination.** On motion of any party in interest supported by an affidavit alleging (1) that the examination of the debtor is necessary for the proper administration of the estate and that there is reasonable cause to believe that the debtor is about to leave or has left the debtor's residence or principal place of business to avoid examination, or (2) that the debtor has evaded service of a subpoena or of an order to attend for examination, or (3) that the debtor has willfully disobeyed a subpoena or order to attend for examination, duly served, the court may issue to the marshal, or some other officer authorized by law, an order directing the officer to bring the debtor before the court without unnecessary delay. If, after hearing, the court finds the allegations to be true, the court shall thereupon cause the debtor to be examined forthwith. If necessary, the court shall fix conditions for further examination and for the debtor's obedience to all orders made in reference thereto.

(b) **Removal.** Whenever any order to bring the debtor before the court is issued under this rule and the debtor is found in a district other than that of the court issuing the order, the debtor may be taken into custody under the order and removed in accordance with the following rules:

   (1) If the debtor is taken into custody under the order at a place less than 100 miles from the place of issue of the order, the debtor shall be brought forthwith before the court that issued the order.

   (2) If the debtor is taken into custody under the order at a place 100 miles or more from the place of issue of the order, the debtor shall be brought without unnecessary delay before the nearest available United States magistrate judge, bankruptcy judge, or district judge. If, after hearing, the magistrate judge, bankruptcy judge, or district judge finds that an order has issued under this rule and that the person in custody is the debtor, or if the person in custody waives a hearing, the magistrate judge, bankruptcy judge, or district judge shall order removal and the person in custody shall be released on conditions ensuring prompt appearance before the court that issued the order to compel the attendance.

(c) **Conditions of Release.** In determining what conditions will reasonably assure attendance or obedience under subdivision (a) of this rule or appearance under subdivision (b) of this rule, the court shall be governed by the provisions and policies of title 18, U.S.C., § 3146(a)and(b).

Rule 2006. Solicitation and Voting of Proxies in Chapter 7 Liquidation Cases

(a) **Applicability.** This rule applies only in a liquidation case pending under chapter 7 of the Code.

(b) **Definitions.**
   (1) *Proxy.* A proxy is a written power of attorney authorizing any entity to vote the claim or otherwise act as the owner's attorney in fact in connection with the administration of the estate.
   (2) *Solicitation of Proxy.* The solicitation of a proxy is any communication, other than one from an attorney to a regular client who owns a claim or from an attorney to the owner of a claim who has requested the attorney to represent the owner, by which a creditor is asked, directly or indirectly, to give a proxy after or in contemplation of the filing of a petition by or against the debtor.

(c) **Authorized Solicitation.**
   (1) A proxy may be solicited only by (A) a creditor owning an allowable unsecured claim against the estate on the date of the filing of the petition; (B) a committee elected pursuant to § 705 of the Code; (C) a committee of creditors selected by a majority in number and amount of claims of creditors (i) whose claims are not contingent or unliquidated, (ii) who are not disqualified from voting under § 702(a) of the Code, and (iii) who were present or represented at a meeting of which all creditors having claims of over $500 or the 100 creditors having the largest claims had at least seven days notice in writing and of which meeting written minutes were kept and are available reporting the names of the creditors present or represented and voting and the amounts of their claims; or (D) a bona fide trade or credit association, but such association may solicit only creditors who were its members or subscribers in good standing and had allowable unsecured claims on the date of the filing of the petition.
   (2) A proxy may be solicited only in writing.

(d) **Solicitation Not Authorized.** This rule does not permit solicitation (1) in any interest other than that of general creditors; (2) by or on behalf of any custodian; (3) by the interim trustee or by or on behalf of any entity not qualified to vote under § 702(a) of the Code; (4) by or on behalf of an attorney at law; or (5) by or on behalf of a transferee of a claim for collection only.

(e) **Data Required from Holders of Multiple Proxies.** At any time before the voting commences at any meeting of creditors pursuant to § 341(a) of the Code, or at any other time as the court may direct, a holder of two or more proxies shall file and transmit to the United States trustee a verified list of the proxies to be voted and a verified statement of the pertinent facts and circumstances in connection with the execution and delivery of each proxy, including:

(1) a copy of the solicitation;

(2) identification of the solicitor, the forwarder, if the forwarder is neither the solicitor nor the owner of the claim, and the proxyholder, including their connections with the debtor and with each other. If the solicitor, forwarder, or proxyholder is an association, there shall also be included a statement that the creditors whose claims have been solicited and the creditors whose claims are to be voted were members or subscribers in good standing and had allowable unsecured claims on the date of the filing of the petition. If the solicitor, forwarder, or proxyholder is a committee of creditors, the statement shall also set forth the date and place the committee was organized, that the committee was organized in accordance with clause (B) or (C) of paragraph (c)(1) of this rule, the members of the committee, the amounts of their claims, when the claims were acquired, the amounts paid therefor, and the extent to which the claims of the committee members are secured or entitled to priority;

(3) a statement that no consideration has been paid or promised by the proxyholder for the proxy;

(4) a statement as to whether there is any agreement and, if so, the particulars thereof, between the proxyholder and any other entity for the payment of any consideration in connection with voting the proxy, or for the sharing of compensation with any entity, other than a member or regular associate of the proxyholder's law firm, which may be allowed the trustee or any entity for services rendered in the case, or for the employment of any person as attorney, accountant, appraiser, auctioneer, or other employee for the estate;

(5) if the proxy was solicited by an entity other than the proxyholder, or forwarded to the holder by an entity who is neither a solicitor of the proxy nor the owner of the claim, a statement signed and verified by the solicitor or forwarder that no consideration has been paid or promised for the proxy, and whether there is any agreement, and, if so, the particulars thereof, between the solicitor or forwarder and any other entity for the payment of any consideration in connection with voting the proxy, or for sharing compensation with any entity other than a member or regular associate of the solicitor's or forwarder's law firm which may be allowed the trustee or any entity for services rendered in the case, or for the employment of any person as attorney, accountant, appraiser, auctioneer, or other employee for the estate;

(6) if the solicitor, forwarder, or proxyholder is a committee, a statement signed and verified by each member as to the amount and source of any consideration paid or to be paid to such member in connection with the case other than by way of dividend on the member's claim.

(f) **Enforcement of Restrictions on Solicitation.** On motion of any party in interest or on its own initiative, the court may determine whether there has been a failure to comply with the provisions of this rule or any other impropriety in connection with the solicitation or voting of a proxy. After notice and a hearing the court may reject any proxy for cause, vacate any order entered in consequence of the voting of any proxy which should have been rejected, or take any other appropriate action.

Rule 2007. Review of Appointment of Creditors' Committee Organized Before Commencement of the Case

(a) **Motion to Review Appointment.** If a committee appointed by the United States trustee pursuant to § 1102(a) of the Code consists of the members of a committee organized by creditors before the commencement of a chapter 9 or chapter 11 case, on motion of a party in interest and after a hearing on notice to the United States trustee and other entities as the court may direct, the court may determine whether the appointment of the committee satisfies the requirements of § 1102(b)(1) of the Code.

(b) **Selection of Members of Committee.** The court may find that a committee organized by unsecured creditors before the commencement of a chapter 9 or chapter 11 case was fairly chosen if:

  (1) it was selected by a majority in number and amount of claims of unsecured creditors who may vote under § 702(a) of the Code and were present in person or represented at a meeting of which all creditors having unsecured claims of over $1,000 or the 100 unsecured creditors having the largest claims had at least seven days notice in writing, and of which meeting written minutes reporting the names of the creditors present or represented and voting and the amounts of their claims were kept and are available for inspection;

  (2) all proxies voted at the meeting for the elected committee were solicited pursuant to Rule 2006 and the lists and statements required by subdivision (e) thereof have been transmitted to the United States trustee; and

  (3) the organization of the committee was in all other respects fair and proper.

(c) **Failure to Comply with Requirements for Appointment.** After a hearing on notice pursuant to subdivision (a) of this rule, the court shall direct the United States trustee to vacate the appointment of the committee and may order other appropriate action if the court finds that such appointment failed to satisfy the requirements of § 1102(b)(1) of the Code.

Rule 2007.1. Appointment of Trustee or Examiner in a Chapter 11 Reorganization Case

(a) **Order to Appoint Trustee or Examiner.** In a chapter 11 reorganization case, a motion for an order to appoint a trustee or an examiner under § 1104(a) or § 1104(c) of the Code shall be made in accordance with Rule 9014.

(b) **Election of Trustee.**

    (1) *Request for an Election.* A request to convene a meeting of creditors for the purpose of electing a trustee in a chapter 11 reorganization case shall be filed and transmitted to the United States trustee in accordance with Rule 5005 within the time prescribed by § 1104(b) of the Code. Pending court approval of the person elected, any person appointed by the United States trustee under § 1104(d) and approved in accordance with subdivision (c) of this rule shall serve as trustee.

    (2) *Manner of Election and Notice.* An election of a trustee under § 1104(b) of Code shall be conducted in the manner provided in Rules 2003(b)(3) and 2006. Notice of the meeting of creditors convened under § 1104(b) shall be given as provided in Rule 2002. The United States trustee shall preside at the meeting. A proxy for the purpose of voting in the election may be solicited only by a committee of creditors appointed under § 1102 of the Code or by any other party entitled to solicit a proxy pursuant to Rule 2006.

    (3) *Report of Election and Resolution of Disputes.*

        (A) Report of Undisputed Election. If no dispute arises out of the election, the United States trustee shall promptly file a report certifying the election, including the name and address of the person elected and a statement that the election is undisputed. The report shall be accompanied by a verified statement of the person elected setting forth that person's connections with the debtor, creditors, any other party in interest, their respective attorneys and accountants, the United States trustee, or any person employed in the office of the United States trustee.

        (B) Dispute Arising Out of an Election. If a dispute arises out of an election, the United States trustee shall promptly file a report stating that the election is disputed, informing the court of the nature of the dispute, and listing the name and address of any candidate elected under any alternative presented by the dispute. The report shall be accompanied by a verified statement by each candidate elected under each alternative presented by the dispute, setting forth the person's connections with the debtor, creditors, any other party in interest, their respective attorneys and accountants, the United States trustee, or any person employed in the office of the United States trustee. Not later than the date on which the report of the disputed election is filed, the United States trustee shall mail a copy of the report and each verified statement to any party in interest that has made a request to convene a meeting under § 1104(b) or to receive a copy of the report, and to any committee appointed under § 1102 of the Code.

(c) **Approval of Appointment.** An order approving the appointment of a trustee or an examiner under § 1104(d) of the Code shall be made on application of the United States trustee. The application shall state the name of the person appointed and, to the best of the applicant's knowledge, all the person's connections with the debtor, creditors, any other parties in interest, their respective attorneys and accountants, the United States trustee, or persons employed in the office of the United States trustee. The application shall state the names of the parties in interest with whom the United States trustee consulted regarding the appointment. The application shall be accompanied by a verified statement of the person appointed setting forth the person's connections with the debtor, creditors, any other party in interest, their respective attorneys and accountants, the United States trustee, or any person employed in the office of the United States trustee.

Rule 2007.2. Appointment of Patient Care Ombudsman in a Health Care Business Case

(a) **Order to Appoint Patient Care Ombudsman.** In a chapter 7, chapter 9, or chapter 11 case in which the debtor is a health care business, the court shall order the appointment of a patient care ombudsman under § 333 of the Code, unless the court, on motion of the United States trustee or a party in interest filed no later than 21 days after the commencement of the case or within another time fixed by the court, finds that the appointment of a patient care ombudsman is not necessary under the specific circumstances of the case for the protection of patients.

(b) **Motion for Order to Appoint Ombudsman.** If the court has found that the appointment of an ombudsman is not necessary, or has terminated the appointment, the court, on motion of the United States trustee or a party in interest, may order the appointment at a later time if it finds that the appointment has become necessary to protect patients.

(c) **Notice of Appointment.** If a patient care ombudsman is appointed under § 333, the United States trustee shall promptly file a notice of the appointment, including the name and address of the person appointed. Unless the person appointed is a State Long-Term Care Ombudsman, the notice shall be accompanied by a verified statement of the person appointed setting forth the person's connections with the debtor, creditors, patients, any other party in interest, their respective attorneys and accountants, the United States trustee, and any person employed in the office of the United States trustee.

(d) **Termination of Appointment.** On motion of the United States trustee or a party in interest, the court may terminate the appointment of a patient care ombudsman if the court finds that the appointment is not necessary to protect patients.

(e) **Motion.** A motion under this rule shall be governed by Rule 9014. The motion shall be transmitted to the United States trustee and served on: the debtor; the trustee; any committee elected under § 705 or appointed under § 1102 of the Code or its authorized agent, or, if the case is a chapter 9 municipality case or a chapter 11 reorganization case and no committee of unsecured creditors has been appointed under § 1102, on the creditors included on the list filed under Rule 1007(d); and such other entities as the court may direct.

Rule 2008. Notice to Trustee of Selection

The United States trustee shall immediately notify the person selected as trustee how to qualify and, if applicable, the amount of the trustee's bond. A trustee that has filed a blanket bond pursuant to Rule 2010 and has been selected as trustee in a chapter 7, chapter 12, or chapter 13 case that does not notify the court and the United States trustee in writing of rejection of the office within seven days after receipt of notice of selection shall be deemed to have accepted the office. Any other person selected as trustee shall notify the court and the United States trustee in writing of acceptance of the office within seven days after receipt of notice of selection or shall be deemed to have rejected the office.

Rule 2009. Trustees for Estates When Joint Administration Ordered

(a) **Election of Single Trustee for Estates Being Jointly Administered.** If the court orders a joint administration of two or more estates under Rule 1015(b), creditors may elect a single trustee for the estates being jointly administered, unless the case is under subchapter V of chapter 7 of the Code.

(b) **Right of Creditors to Elect Separate Trustee.** Notwithstanding entry of an order for joint administration under Rule 1015(b), the creditors of any debtor may elect a separate trustee for the estate of the debtor as provided in § 702 of the Code, unless the case is under subchapter V of chapter 7.

(c) **Appointment of Trustees for Estates Being Jointly Administered.**

(1) *Chapter 7 Liquidation Cases.* Except in a case governed by subchapter V of chapter 7, the United States trustee may appoint one or more interim trustees for estates being jointly administered in chapter 7 cases.

(2) *Chapter 11 Reorganization Cases.* If the appointment of a trustee is ordered, the United States trustee may appoint one or more trustees for estates being jointly administered in chapter 11 cases.

(3) *Chapter 12 Family Farmer's Debt Adjustment Cases.* The United States trustee may appoint one or more trustees for estates being jointly administered in chapter 12 cases.

    (4) *Chapter 13 Individual's Debt Adjustment Cases.* The United States trustee may appoint one or more trustees for estates being jointly administered in chapter 13 cases.

(d) **Potential Conflicts of Interest.** On a showing that creditors or equity security holders of the different estates will be prejudiced by conflicts of interest of a common trustee who has been elected or appointed, the court shall order the selection of separate trustees for estates being jointly administered.

(e) **Separate Accounts.** The trustee or trustees of estates being jointly administered shall keep separate accounts of the property and distribution of each estate.

Rule 2010. Qualification by Trustee; Proceeding on Bond

(a) **Blanket Bond.** The United States trustee may authorize a blanket bond in favor of the United States conditioned on the faithful performance of official duties by the trustee or trustees to cover (1) a person who qualifies as trustee in a number of cases, and (2) a number of trustees each of whom qualifies in a different case.

(b) **Proceeding on Bond.** A proceeding on the trustee's bond may be brought by any party in interest in the name of the United States for the use of the entity injured by the breach of the condition.

Rule 2011. Evidence of Debtor in Possession or Qualification of Trustee

(a) Whenever evidence is required that a debtor is a debtor in possession or that a trustee has qualified, the clerk may so certify and the certificate shall constitute conclusive evidence of that fact.

(b) If a person elected or appointed as trustee does not qualify within the time prescribed by § 322(a) of the Code, the clerk shall so notify the court and the United States trustee.

Rule 2012. Substitution of Trustee or Successor Trustee; Accounting

(a) **Trustee.** If a trustee is appointed in a chapter 11 case or the debtor is removed as debtor in possession in a chapter 12 case, the trustee is substituted automatically for the debtor in possession as a party in any pending action, proceeding, or matter.

(b) **Successor Trustee.** When a trustee dies, resigns, is removed, or otherwise ceases to hold office during the pendency of a case under the Code (1) the successor is automatically substituted as a party in any pending action, proceeding, or matter; and (2) the successor trustee shall prepare, file, and transmit to the United States trustee an accounting of the prior administration of the estate.

Rule 2013. Public Record of Compensation Awarded to Trustees, Examiners, and Professionals

(a) **Record to Be Kept.** The clerk shall maintain a public record listing fees awarded by the court (1) to trustees and attorneys, accountants, appraisers, auctioneers and other professionals employed by trustees, and (2) to examiners. The record shall include the name and docket number of the case, the name of the individual or firm receiving the fee and the amount of the fee awarded. The record shall be maintained chronologically and shall be kept current and open to examination by the public without charge. "Trustees," as used in this rule, does not include debtors in possession.

(b) **Summary of Record.** At the close of each annual period, the clerk shall prepare a summary of the public record by individual or firm name, to reflect total fees awarded during the preceding year. The summary shall be open to examination by the public without charge. The clerk shall transmit a copy of the summary to the United States trustee.

Rule 2014. Employment of Professional Persons

(a) **Application for an Order of Employment.** An order approving the employment of attorneys, accountants, appraisers, auctioneers, agents, or other professionals pursuant to § 327, § 1103, or § 1114 of the Code shall be made only on application of the trustee or committee. The application shall be filed and, unless the case is a chapter 9 municipality case, a copy of the application shall be transmitted by the applicant to the United States trustee. The application shall state the specific facts showing the necessity for the employment, the name of the person to be employed, the reasons for the selection, the professional services to be rendered, any proposed arrangement for compensation, and, to the best of the applicant's knowledge, all of the person's connections with the debtor, creditors, any other party in interest, their respective attorneys and accountants, the United States trustee, or any person employed in the office of the United States trustee. The application shall be accompanied by a verified statement of the person to be employed setting forth the person's connections with the debtor, creditors, any other party in interest, their respective attorneys and accountants, the United States trustee, or any person employed in the office of the United States trustee.

(b) **Services Rendered by Member or Associate of Firm of Attorneys or Accountants.** If, under the Code and this rule, a law partnership or corporation is employed as an attorney, or an accounting partnership or corporation is employed as an accountant, or if a named attorney or accountant is employed, any partner, member, or regular associate of the partnership, corporation or individual may act as attorney or accountant so employed, without further order of the court.

Rule 2015. Duty to Keep Records, Make Reports, and Give Notice of Case or Change of Status

(a) **Trustee or Debtor in Possession.** A trustee or debtor in possession shall:

    (1) in a chapter 7 liquidation case and, if the court directs, in a chapter 11 reorganization case file and transmit to the United States trustee a complete inventory of the property of the debtor within 30 days after qualifying as a trustee or debtor in possession, unless such an inventory has already been filed;

    (2) keep a record of receipts and the disposition of money and property received;

    (3) file the reports and summaries required by § 704(a)(8) of the Code, which shall include a statement, if payments are made to employees, of the amounts of deductions for all taxes required to be withheld or paid for and in behalf of employees and the place where these amounts are deposited;

    (4) as soon as possible after the commencement of the case, give notice of the case to every entity known to be holding money or property subject to withdrawal or order of the debtor, including every bank, savings or building and loan association, public utility company, and landlord with whom the ebtor has a deposit, and to every insurance company which has issued a policy having a cash surrender value payable to the debtor, except that notice need not be given to any entity who has knowledge or has previously been notified of the case;

    (5) in a chapter 11 reorganization case, on or before the last day of the month after each calendar quarter during which there is a duty to pay fees under28 U.S.C. § 1930(a)(6), file and transmit to the United States trustee a statement of any disbursements made during that quarter and of any fees payable under 28 U.S.C. § 1930(a)(6) for that quarter; and

    (6) in a chapter 11 small business case, unless the court, for cause, sets another reporting interval, file and transmit to the United States trustee for each calendar month after the order for relief, on the appropriate Official Form, the report required by § 308. If the order for relief is within the first 15 days of a calendar month, a report shall be filed for the portion of the month that follows the order for relief. If the order for relief is after the 15th day of a calendar month, the period for the remainder of the month shall be included in the report for the next calendar month. Each report shall be filed no later than 21 days after the last day of the calendar month following the month covered by the report. The obligation to file reports under this subparagraph terminates on the effective date of the plan, or conversion or dismissal of the case.

(b) **Chapter 12 Trustee and Debtor in Possession.** In a chapter 12 family farmer's debt adjustment case, the debtor in possession shall perform the duties prescribed in clauses (2)-(4) of subdivision (a) of this rule and, if the court directs, shall file and transmit to the United States trustee a complete inventory of the property of the debtor within the time fixed by the court. If the debtor is removed as debtor in possession, the trustee shall perform the duties of the debtor in possession prescribed in this paragraph.

(c) **Chapter 13 Trustee and Debtor.**

   (1) *Business Cases.* In a chapter 13 individual's debt adjustment case, when the debtor is engaged in business, the debtor shall perform the duties prescribed by clauses (2)-(4) of subdivision (a) of this rule and, if the court directs, shall file and transmit to the United States trustee a complete inventory of the property of the debtor within the time fixed by the court.

   (2) *Nonbusiness Cases.* In a chapter 13 individual's debt adjustment case, when the debtor is not engaged in business, the trustee shall perform the duties prescribed by clause (2) of subdivision (a) of this rule.

(d) **Foreign Representative.** In a case in which the court has granted recognition of a foreign proceeding under chapter 15, the foreign representative shall file any notice required under § 1518 of the Code within 14 days after the date when the representative becomes aware of the subsequent information.

(e) **Transmission of Reports.** In a chapter 11 case the court may direct that copies or summaries of annual reports and copies or summaries of other reports shall be mailed to the creditors, equity security holders, and indenture trustees. The court may also direct the publication of summaries of any such reports. A copy of every report or summary mailed or published pursuant to this subdivision shall be transmitted to the United States trustee.

Rule 2015.1. Patient Care Ombudsman

(a) Reports. A patient care ombudsman, at least 14 days before making a report under § 333(b)(2) of the Code, shall give notice that the report will be made to the court, unless the court orders otherwise. The notice shall be transmitted to the United States trustee, posted conspicuously at the health care facility that is the subject of the report, and served on: the debtor; the trustee; all patients; and any committee elected under § 705 or appointed under § 1102 of the Code or its authorized agent, or, if the case is a chapter 9 municipality case or a chapter 11 reorganization case and no committee of unsecured creditors has been appointed under § 1102, on the creditors included on the list filed under Rule 1007(d); and such other entities as the court may direct. The notice shall state the date and time when the report will be made, the manner in which the report will be made, and, if the report is in writing, the name, address, telephone number, email address, and website, if any, of the person from whom a copy of the report may be obtained at the debtor's expense.

(b) Authorization to Review Confidential Patient Records. A motion by a patient care ombudsman under § 333(c) to review confidential patient records shall be governed by Rule 9014, served on the patient and any family member or other contact person whose name and address have been given to the trustee or the debtor for the purpose of providing information regarding the patient's health care, and transmitted to the United States trustee subject to applicable nonbankruptcy law relating to patient privacy. Unless the court orders otherwise, a hearing on the motion may not be commenced earlier than 14 days after service of the motion.

Rule 2015.2. Transfer of Patient in Health Care Business Case

Unless the court orders otherwise, if the debtor is a health care business, the trustee may not transfer a patient to another health care business under § 704(a)(12) of the Code unless the trustee gives at least 14 days' notice of the transfer to the patient care ombudsman, if any, the patient, and any family member or other contact person whose name and address have been given to the trustee or the debtor for the purpose of providing information regarding the patient's health care. The notice is subject to applicable nonbankruptcy law relating to patient privacy.

Rule 2015.3. Reports of Financial Information on Entities in Which a Chapter 11 Estate Holds a Controlling or Substantial Interest

(a) **Reporting Requirement.** In a chapter 11 case, the trustee or debtor in possession shall file periodic financial reports of the value, operations, and profitability of each entity that is not a publicly traded corporation or a debtor in a case under title 11, and in which the estate holds a substantial or controlling interest. The reports shall be prepared as prescribed by the appropriate Official Form, and shall be based upon the most recent information reasonably available to the trustee or debtor in possession.

(b) **Time for Filing; Service.** The first report required by this rule shall be filed no later than seven days before the first date set for the meeting of creditors under § 341 of the Code. Subsequent reports shall be filed no less frequently than every six months thereafter, until the effective date of a plan or the case is dismissed or converted. Copies of the report shall be served on the United States trustee, any committee appointed under § 1102 of the Code, and any other party in interest that has filed a request therefor.

(c) **Presumption of Substantial or Controlling Interest; Judicial Determination.** For purposes of this rule, an entity of which the estate controls or owns at least a 20 percent interest, shall be presumed to be an entity in which the estate has a substantial or controlling interest. An entity in which the estate controls or owns less than a 20 percent interest shall be presumed not to be an entity in which the estate has a substantial or controlling interest. Upon motion, the entity, any holder of an interest therein, the United States trustee, or any other party in interest may seek to rebut either presumption, and the court shall, after notice and a hearing, determine whether the estate's interest in the entity is substantial or controlling.

(d) **Modification of Reporting Requirement.** The court may, after notice and a hearing, vary the reporting requirement established by subdivision (a) of this rule for cause, including that the trustee or debtor in possession is not able, after a good faith effort, to comply with those reporting requirements, or that the information required by subdivision (a) is publicly available.

(e) **Notice and Protective Orders.** No later than 14 days before filing the first report required by this rule, the trustee or debtor in possession shall send notice to the entity in which the estate has a substantial or controlling interest, and to all holders—known to the trustee or debtor in possession—of an interest in that entity, that the trustee or debtor in possession expects to file and serve financial information relating to the entity in accordance with this rule. The entity in which the estate has a substantial or controlling interest, or a person holding an interest in that entity, may request protection of the information under § 107 of the Code.

(f) Effect of Request. Unless the court orders otherwise, the pendency of a request under subdivisions (c), (d), or (e) of this rule shall not alter or stay the requirements of subdivision (a).

Rule 2016. Compensation for Services Rendered and Reimbursement of Expenses

(a) **Application for Compensation or Reimbursement.** An entity seeking interim or final compensation for services, or reimbursement of necessary expenses, from the estate shall file an application setting forth a detailed statement of (1) the services rendered, time expended and expenses incurred, and (2) the amounts requested. An application for compensation shall include a statement as to what payments have theretofore been made or promised to the applicant for services rendered or to be rendered in any capacity whatsoever in connection with the case, the source of the compensation so paid or promised, whether any compensation previously received has been shared and whether an agreement or understanding exists between the applicant and any other entity for the sharing of compensation received or to be received for services rendered in or in connection with the case, and the particulars of any sharing of compensation or agreement or understanding therefor, except that details of any agreement by the applicant for the sharing of compensation as a member or regular associate of a firm of lawyers or accountants shall not be required. The requirements of this subdivision shall apply to an application for compensation for services rendered by an attorney or accountant even though the application is filed by a creditor or other entity. Unless the case is a chapter 9 municipality case, the applicant shall transmit to the United States trustee a copy of the application.

(b) **Disclosure of Compensation Paid or Promised to Attorney for Debtor**. Every attorney for a debtor, whether or not the attorney applies for compensation, shall file and transmit to the United States trustee within 14 days after the order for relief, or at another time as the court may direct, the statement required by § 329 of the Code including whether the attorney has shared or agreed to share the compensation with any other entity. The statement shall include the particulars of any such sharing or agreement to share by the attorney, but the details of any agreement for the sharing of the compensation with a member or regular associate of the attorney's law firm shall not be required. A supplemental statement shall be filed and transmitted to the United States trustee within 14 days after any payment or agreement not previously disclosed.

(c) **Disclosure of Compensation Paid or Promised to Bankruptcy Petition Preparer**. Before a petition is filed, every bankruptcy petition preparer for a debtor shall deliver to the debtor, the declaration under penalty of perjury required by § 110(h)(2). The declaration shall disclose any fee, and the source of any fee, received from or on behalf of the debtor within 12 months of the filing of the case and all unpaid fees charged to the debtor. The declaration shall also describe the services performed and documents prepared or caused to be prepared by the bankruptcy petition preparer. The declaration shall be filed with the petition. The petition preparer shall file a supplemental statement within 14 days after any payment or agreement not previously disclosed.

Rule 2017. Examination of Debtor's Transactions with Debtor's Attorney

(a) **Payment or Transfer to Attorney Before Order for Relief**. On motion by any party in interest or on the court's own initiative, the court after notice and a hearing may determine whether any payment of money or any transfer of property by the debtor, made directly or indirectly and in contemplation of the filing of a petition under the Code by or against the debtor or before entry of the order for relief in an involuntary case, to an attorney for services rendered or to be rendered is excessive.

(b) **Payment or Transfer to Attorney After Order for Relief**. On motion by the debtor, the United States trustee or on the court's own initiative, the court after notice and a hearing may determine whether any payment of money or any transfer of property, or any agreement therefor, by the debtor to an attorney after entry of an order for relief in a case under the Code is excessive, whether the payment or transfer is made or is to be made directly or indirectly, if the payment, transfer, or agreement therefor is for services in any way related to the case.

Rule 2018. Intervention; Right to Be Heard

(a) **Permissive Intervention**. In a case under the Code, after hearing on such notice as the court directs and for cause shown, the court may permit any interested entity to intervene generally or with respect to any specified matter.

(b) **Intervention by Attorney General of a State**. In a chapter 7, 11, 12, or 13 case, the Attorney General of a State may appear and be heard on behalf of consumer creditors if the court determines the appearance is in the public interest, but the Attorney General may not appeal from any judgment, order, or decree in the case.

(c) **Chapter 9 Municipality Case**. The Secretary of the Treasury of the United States may, or if requested by the court shall, intervene in a chapter 9 case. Representatives of the state in which the debtor is located may intervene in a chapter 9 case with respect to matters specified by the court.

(d) **Labor Unions**. In a chapter 9, 11, or 12 case, a labor union or employees' association, representative of employees of the debtor, shall have the right to be heard on the economic soundness of a plan affecting the interests of the employees. A labor union or employees' association which exercises its right to be heard under this subdivision shall not be entitled to appeal any judgment, order, or decree relating to the plan, unless otherwise permitted by law.

(e) **Service on Entities Covered by This Rule**. The court may enter orders governing the service of notice and papers on entities permitted to intervene or be heard pursuant to this rule.

Rule 2019. Disclosure Regarding Creditors and Equity Security Holders in Chapter 9 and Chapter 11 Cases

(a) **Definitions**. In this rule the following terms have the meanings indicated:
    (1) "Disclosable economic interest" means any claim, interest, pledge, lien, option, participation, derivative instrument, or any other right or derivative right granting the holder an economic interest that is affected by the value, acquisition, or disposition of a claim or interest.
    (2) "Represent" or "represents" means to take a position before the court or to solicit votes regarding the confirmation of a plan on behalf of another.

(b) **Disclosure by Groups, Committees, and Entities**.
    (1) In a chapter 9 or 11 case, a verified statement setting forth the information specified in subdivision (c) of this rule shall be filed by every group or committee that consists of or represents, and every entity that represents, multiple creditors or equity security holders that are
        (A) acting in concert to advance their common interests, and
        (B) not composed entirely of affiliates or insiders of one another.
    (2) Unless the court orders otherwise, an entity is not required to file the verified statement described in paragraph (1) of this subdivision solely because of its status as:
        (A) an indenture trustee;

       (B) an agent for one or more other entities under an agreement for the extension of credit;

       (C) a class action representative; or

       (D) a governmental unit that is not a person.

(c) **Information Required**. The verified statement shall include:

   (1) the pertinent facts and circumstances concerning:

       (A) with respect to a group or committee, other than a committee appointed under § 1102 or § 1114 of the Code, the formation of the group or committee, including the name of each entity at whose instance the group or committee was formed or for whom the group or committee has agreed to act; or

       (B) with respect to an entity, the employment of the entity, including the name of each creditor or equity security holder at whose instance the employment was arranged;

   (2) if not disclosed under subdivision (c)(1), with respect to an entity, and with respect to each member of a group or committee:

       (A) name and address;

       (B) the nature and amount of each disclosable economic interest held in relation to the debtor as of the date the entity was employed or the group or committee was formed; and

       (C) with respect to each member of a group or committee that claims to represent any entity in addition to the members of the group or committee, other than a committee appointed under § 1102 or § 1114 of the Code, the date of acquisition by quarter and year of each disclosable economic interest, unless acquired more than one year before the petition was filed;

   (3) if not disclosed under subdivision (c)(1) or (c)(2), with respect to each creditor or equity security holder represented by an entity, group, or committee, other than a committee appointed under § 1102 or § 1114 of the Code:

       (A) name and address; and

       (B) the nature and amount of each disclosable economic interest held in relation to the debtor as of the date of the statement; and

   (4) a copy of the instrument, if any, authorizing the entity, group, or committee to act on behalf of creditors or equity security holders.

(d) **Supplemental Statements**. If any fact disclosed in its most recently filed statement has changed materially, an entity, group, or committee shall file a verified supplemental statement whenever it takes a position before the court or solicits votes on the confirmation of a plan. The supplemental statement shall set forth the material changes in the facts required by subdivision (c) to be disclosed.

(e) **Determination of Failure to Comply; Sanctions**.

   (1) On motion of any party in interest, or on its own motion, the court may determine whether there has been a failure to comply with any provision of this rule.

(2) If the court finds such a failure to comply, it may:
    (A) refuse to permit the entity, group, or committee to be heard or to intervene in the case;
    (B) hold invalid any authority, acceptance, rejection, or objection given, procured, or received by the entity, group, or committee; or
    (C) grant other appropriate relief.

Rule 2020. Review of Acts by United States Trustee

A proceeding to contest any act or failure to act by the United States trustee is governed by Rule 9014.

Part III. Claims and distribution to creditors and equity interest holders; plans

Rule 3001. Proof of Claim

(a) **Form and Content**. A proof of claim is a written statement setting forth a creditor's claim. A proof of claim shall conform substantially to the appropriate Official Form.

(b) **Who May Execute**. A proof of claim shall be executed by the creditor or the creditor's authorized agent except as provided in Rules 3004 and 3005.

(c) **Supporting Information**.

    (1) *Claim Based on a Writing.* Except for a claim governed by paragraph (3) of this subdivision, when a claim, or an interest in property of the debtor securing the claim, is based on a writing, a copy of the writing shall be filed with the proof of claim. If the writing has been lost or destroyed, a statement of the circumstances of the loss or destruction shall be filed with the claim.

    (2) *Additional Requirements in an Individual Debtor Case; Sanctions for Failure to Comply.* In a case in which the debtor is an individual:

        (A) If, in addition to its principal amount, a claim includes interest, fees, expenses, or other charges incurred before the petition was filed, an itemized statement of the interest, fees, expenses, or charges shall be filed with the proof of claim.

        (B) If a security interest is claimed in the debtor's property, a statement of the amount necessary to cure any default as of the date of the petition shall be filed with the proof of claim.

        (C) If a security interest is claimed in property that is the debtor's principal residence, the attachment prescribed by the appropriate Official Form shall be filed with the proof of claim. If an escrow account has been established in connection with the claim, an escrow account statement prepared as of the date the petition was filed and in a form consistent with applicable nonbankruptcy law shall be filed with the attachment to the proof of claim.

        (D) If the holder of a claim fails to provide any information required by this subdivision (c), the court may, after notice and hearing, take either or both of the following actions:

            (i) preclude the holder from presenting the omitted information, in any form, as evidence in any contested matter or adversary proceeding in the case, unless the court determines that the failure was substantially justified or is harmless; or

            (ii) award other appropriate relief, including reasonable expenses and attorney's fees caused by the failure.

    (3) *Claim Based on an Open-End or Revolving Consumer Credit Agreement.*

    (A) When a claim is based on an open-end or revolving consumer credit agreement—except one for which a security interest is claimed in the debtor's real property—a statement shall be filed with the proof of claim, including all of the following information that applies to the account:

        (i)   the name of the entity from whom the creditor purchased the account;

        (ii) the name of the entity to whom the debt was owed at the time of an account holder's last transaction on the account;

        (iii) the date of an account holder's last transaction;

        (iv) the date of the last payment on the account; and

        (v) the date on which the account was charged to profit and loss.

    (B) On written request by a party in interest, the holder of a claim based on an open-end or revolving consumer credit agreement shall, within 30 days after the request is sent, provide the requesting party a copy of the writing specified in paragraph (1) of this subdivision.

(d) **Evidence of Perfection of Security Interest**. If a security interest in property of the debtor is claimed, the proof of claim shall be accompanied by evidence that the security interest has been perfected.

(e) **Transferred Claim.**

    (1) *Transfer of Claim Other Than for Security Before Proof Filed*. If a claim has been transferred other than for security before proof of the claim has been filed, the proof of claim may be filed only by the transferee or an indenture trustee.

    (2) *Transfer of Claim Other than for Security after Proof Filed*. If a claim other than one based on a publicly traded note, bond, or debenture has been transferred other than for security after the proof of claim has been filed, evidence of the transfer shall be filed by the transferee. The clerk shall immediately notify the alleged transferor by mail of the filing of the evidence of transfer and that objection thereto, if any, must be filed within 21 days of the mailing of the notice or within any additional time allowed by the court. If the alleged transferor files a timely objection and the court finds, after notice and a hearing, that the claim has been transferred other than for security, it shall enter an order substituting the transferee for the transferor. If a timely objection is not filed by the alleged transferor, the transferee shall be substituted for the transferor.

    (3) *Transfer of Claim for Security Before Proof Filed*. If a claim other than one based on a publicly traded note, bond, or debenture has been transferred for security before proof of the claim has been filed, the transferor or transferee or both may file a proof of claim for the full amount. The proof shall be supported by a statement setting forth the terms of the transfer. If either the transferor or the transferee files a proof of claim, the clerk shall immediately notify the other by mail of the right to join in the filed claim. If both transferor and transferee file proofs of the same claim, the proofs shall be consolidated. If the

transferor or transferee does not file an agreement regarding its relative rights respecting voting of the claim, payment of dividends thereon, or participation in the administration of the estate, on motion by a party in interest and after notice and a hearing, the court shall enter such orders respecting these matters as may be appropriate.

(4) *Transfer of Claim for Security after Proof Filed.* If a claim other than one based on a publicly traded note, bond, or debenture has been transferred for security after the proof of claim has been filed, evidence of the terms of the transfer shall be filed by the transferee. The clerk shall immediately notify the alleged transferor by mail of the filing of the evidence of transfer and that objection thereto, if any, must be filed within 21 days of the mailing of the notice or within any additional time allowed by the court. If a timely objection is filed by the alleged transferor, the court, after notice and a hearing, shall determine whether the claim has been transferred for security. If the transferor or transferee does not file an agreement regarding its relative rights respecting voting of the claim, payment of dividends thereon, or participation in the administration of the estate, on motion by a party in interest and after notice and a hearing, the court shall enter such orders respecting these matters as may be appropriate.

(5) *Service of Objection or Motion; Notice of Hearing.* A copy of an objection filed pursuant to paragraph (2) or (4) or a motion filed pursuant to paragraph (3) or (4) of this subdivision together with a notice of a hearing shall be mailed or otherwise delivered to the transferor or transferee, whichever is appropriate, at least 30 days prior to the hearing.

(f) **Evidentiary Effect.** A proof of claim executed and filed in accordance with these rules shall constitute prima facie evidence of the validity and amount of the claim.

(g) To the extent not inconsistent with the United States Warehouse Act or applicable State law, a warehouse receipt, scale ticket, or similar document of the type routinely issued as evidence of title by a grain storage facility, as defined in section 557 of title 11, shall constitute prima facie evidence of the validity and amount of a claim of ownership of a quantity of grain.

Rule 3002. Filing Proof of Claim or Interest

(a) **Necessity for Filing.** A secured creditor, unsecured creditor, or equity security holder must file a proof of claim or interest for the claim or interest to be allowed, except as provided in Rules 1019(3), 3003, 3004, and 3005. A lien that secures a claim against the debtor is not void due only to the failure of any entity to file a proof of claim.

(b) **Place of Filing.** A proof of claim or interest shall be filed in accordance with Rule 5005.

(c) **Time for Filing**. In a voluntary chapter 7 case, chapter 12 case, or chapter 13 case, a proof of claim is timely filed if it is filed not later than 70 days after the order for relief under that chapter or the date of the order of conversion to a case under chapter 12 or chapter 13. In an involuntary chapter 7 case, a proof of claim is timely filed if it is filed not later than 90 days after the order for relief under that chapter is entered. But in all these cases, the following exceptions apply:

(1) A proof of claim filed by a governmental unit, other than for a claim resulting from a tax return filed under § 1308, is timely filed if it is filed not later than 180 days after the date of the order for relief. A proof of claim filed by a governmental unit for a claim resulting from a tax return filed under § 1308 is timely filed if it is filed no later than 180 days after the date of the order for relief or 60 days after the date of the filing of the tax return. The court may, for cause, enlarge the time for a governmental unit to file a proof of claim only upon motion of the governmental unit made before expiration of the period for filing a timely proof of claim.

(2) In the interest of justice and if it will not unduly delay the administration of the case, the court may extend the time for filing a proof of claim by an infant or incompetent person or the representative of either.

(3) An unsecured claim which arises in favor of an entity or becomes allowable as a result of a judgment may be filed within 30 days after the judgment becomes final if the judgment is for the recovery of money or property from that entity or denies or avoids the entity's interest in property. If the judgment imposes a liability which is not satisfied, or a duty which is not performed within such period or such further time as the court may permit, the claim shall not be allowed.

(4) A claim arising from the rejection of an executory contract or unexpired lease of the debtor may be filed within such time as the court may direct.

(5) If notice of insufficient assets to pay a dividend was given to creditors under Rule 2002(e), and subsequently the trustee notifies the court that payment of a dividend appears possible, the clerk shall give at least 90 days' notice by mail to creditors of that fact and of the date by which proofs of claim must be filed.

(6) On motion filed by a creditor before or after the expiration of the time to file a proof of claim, the court may extend the time by not more than 60 days from the date of the order granting the motion. The motion may be granted if the court finds that:

(A) the notice was insufficient under the circumstances to give the creditor a reasonable time to file a proof of claim because the debtor failed to timely file the list of creditors' names and addresses required by Rule 1007(a); or

(B) the notice was insufficient under the circumstances to give the creditor a reasonable time to file a proof of claim, and the notice was mailed to the creditor at a foreign address.

   (7) A proof of claim filed by the holder of a claim that is secured by a security interest in the debtor's principal residence is timely filed if:

      (A) the proof of claim, together with the attachments required by Rule 3001(c)(2)(C), is filed not later than 70 days after the order for relief is entered; and

      (B) any attachments required by Rule 3001(c)(1) and (d) are filed as a supplement to the holder's claim not later than 120 days after the order for relief is entered.

Rule 3002.1. Notice Relating to Claims Secured by Security Interest in the Debtor's Principal Residence

(a) **In General.** This rule applies in a chapter 13 case to claims (1) that are secured by a security interest in the debtor's principal residence, and (2) for which the plan provides that either the trustee or the debtor will make contractual installment payments. Unless the court orders otherwise, the notice requirements of this rule cease to apply when an order terminating or annulling the automatic stay becomes effective with respect to the residence that secures the claim.

(b) **Notice of Payment Changes.** The holder of the claim shall file and serve on the debtor, debtor's counsel, and the trustee a notice of any change in the payment amount, including any change that results from an interest rate or escrow account adjustment, no later than 21 days before a payment in the new amount is due.

(c) **Notice of Fees, Expenses, and Charges.** The holder of the claim shall file and serve on the debtor, debtor's counsel, and the trustee a notice itemizing all fees, expenses, or charges (1) that were incurred in connection with the claim after the bankruptcy case was filed, and (2) that the holder asserts are recoverable against the debtor or against the debtor's principal residence. The notice shall be served within 180 days after the date on which the fees, expenses, or charges are incurred.

(d) **Form and Content.** A notice filed and served under subdivision (b) or (c) of this rule shall be prepared as prescribed by the appropriate Official Form, and filed as a supplement to the holder's proof of claim. The notice is not subject to Rule 3001(f).

(e) **Determination of Fees, Expenses, or Charges.** On motion of the debtor or trustee filed within one year after service of a notice under subdivision (c) of this rule, the court shall, after notice and hearing, determine whether payment of any claimed fee, expense, or charge is required by the underlying agreement and applicable nonbankruptcy law to cure a default or maintain payments in accordance with § 1322(b)(5) of the Code.

(f) **Notice of Final Cure Payment.** Within 30 days after the debtor completes all payments under the plan, the trustee shall file and serve on the holder of the claim, the debtor, and debtor's counsel a notice stating that the debtor has paid in full the amount required to cure any default on the claim. The notice shall also inform the holder of its obligation to file and serve a response under subdivision (g). If the debtor contends that final cure payment has been made and all plan payments have been completed, and the trustee does not timely file and serve the notice required by this subdivision, the debtor may file and serve the notice.

(g) **Response to Notice of Final Cure Payment.** Within 21 days after service of the notice under subdivision (f) of this rule, the holder shall file and serve on the debtor, debtor's counsel, and the trustee a statement indicating (1) whether it agrees that the debtor has paid in full the amount required to cure the default on the claim, and (2) whether the debtor is otherwise current on all payments consistent with § 1322(b)(5) of the Code. The statement shall itemize the required cure or postpetition amounts, if any, that the holder contends remain unpaid as of the date of the statement. The statement shall be filed as a supplement to the holder's proof of claim and is not subject to Rule 3001(f).

(h) **Determination of Final Cure and Payment.** On motion of the debtor or trustee filed within 21 days after service of the statement under subdivision (g) of this rule, the court shall, after notice and hearing, determine whether the debtor has cured the default and paid all required postpetition amounts.

(i) **Failure to Notify.** If the holder of a claim fails to provide any information as required by subdivision (b), (c), or (g) of this rule, the court may, after notice and hearing, take either or both of the following actions:

    (1) preclude the holder from presenting the omitted information, in any form, as evidence in any contested matter or adversary proceeding in the case, unless the court determines that the failure was substantially justified or is harmless; or

    (2) award other appropriate relief, including reasonable expenses and attorney's fees caused by the failure.

Rule 3003. Filing Proof of Claim or Equity Security Interest in Chapter 9 Municipality or Chapter 11 Reorganization Cases

(a) **Applicability of Rule.** This rule applies in chapter 9 and 11 cases.

(b) **Schedule of Liabilities and List of Equity Security Holders.**

    (1) *Schedule of Liabilities.* The schedule of liabilities filed pursuant to § 521(1) of the Code shall constitute prima facie evidence of the validity and amount of the claims of creditors, unless they are scheduled as disputed, contingent, or unliquidated. It shall not be necessary for a creditor or equity security holder to file a proof of claim or interest except as provided in subdivision (c)(2) of this rule.

    (2) *List of Equity Security Holders.* The list of equity security holders filed pursuant to Rule 1007(a)(3) shall constitute prima facie evidence of the validity and amount of the equity security interests and it shall not be necessary for the holders of such interests to file a proof of interest.

(c) **Filing Proof of Claim.**

(1) *Who May File.* Any creditor or indenture trustee may file a proof of claim within the time prescribed by subdivision (c)(3) of this rule.

(2) *Who Must File.* Any creditor or equity security holder whose claim or interest is not scheduled or scheduled as disputed, contingent, or unliquidated shall file a proof of claim or interest within the time prescribed by subdivision (c)(3) of this rule; any creditor who fails to do so shall not be treated as a creditor with respect to such claim for the purposes of voting and distribution.

(3) *Time for Filing.* The court shall fix and for cause shown may extend the time within which proofs of claim or interest may be filed. Notwithstanding the expiration of such time, a proof of claim may be filed to the extent and under the conditions stated in Rule 3002(c)(2), (c)(3), (c)(4), and (c)(6).

(4) *Effect of Filing Claim or Interest.* A proof of claim or interest executed and filed in accordance with this subdivision shall supersede any scheduling of that claim or interest pursuant to § 521(a)(1) of the Code.

(5) *Filing by Indenture Trustee.* An indenture trustee may file a claim on behalf of all known or unknown holders of securities issued pursuant to the trust instrument under which it is trustee.

(d) **Proof of Right to Record Status**. For the purposes of Rules 3017, 3018 and 3021 and for receiving notices, an entity who is not the record holder of a security may file a statement setting forth facts which entitle that entity to be treated as the record holder. An objection to the statement may be filed by any party in interest.

Rule 3004. Filing of Claims by Debtor or Trustee

If a creditor does not timely file a proof of claim under Rule 3002(c) or 3003(c), the debtor or trustee may file a proof of the claim within 30 days after the expiration of the time for filing claims prescribed by Rule 3002(c) or 3003(c), whichever is applicable. The clerk shall forthwith give notice of the filing to the creditor, the debtor and the trustee.

Rule 3005. Filing of Claim, Acceptance, or Rejection by Guarantor, Surety, Indorser, or Other Codebtor

(a) **Filing of Claim**. If a creditor does not timely file a proof of claim under Rule 3002(c) or 3003(c), any entity that is or may be liable with the debtor to that creditor, or who has secured that creditor, may file a proof of the claim within 30 days after the expiration of the time for filing claims prescribed by Rule 3002(c) or Rule 3003(c) whichever is applicable. No distribution shall be made on the claim except on satisfactory proof that the original debt will be diminished by the amount of distribution.

(b) **Filing of Acceptance or Rejection; Substitution of Creditor**. An entity which has filed a claim pursuant to the first sentence of subdivision (a) of this rule may file an acceptance or rejection of a plan in the name of the creditor, if known, or if unknown, in the entity's own name but if the creditor files a proof of claim within the time permitted by Rule 3003(c) or files a notice prior to confirmation of a plan of the creditor's intention to act in the creditor's own behalf, the creditor shall be substituted for the obligor with respect to that claim.

Rule 3006. Withdrawal of Claim; Effect on Acceptance or Rejection of Plan

A creditor may withdraw a claim as of right by filing a notice of withdrawal, except as provided in this rule. If after a creditor has filed a proof of claim an objection is filed thereto or a complaint is filed against that creditor in an adversary proceeding, or the creditor has accepted or rejected the plan or otherwise has participated significantly in the case, the creditor may not withdraw the claim except on order of the court after a hearing on notice to the trustee or debtor in possession, and any creditors' committee elected pursuant to § 705(a) or appointed pursuant to § 1102 of the Code. The order of the court shall contain such terms and conditions as the court deems proper. Unless the court orders otherwise, an authorized withdrawal of a claim shall constitute withdrawal of any related acceptance or rejection of a plan.

Rule 3007. Objections to Claims

(a) **Time and Manner of Service**.
   (1) *Time of Service*. An objection to the allowance of a claim and a notice of objection that substantially conforms to the appropriate Official Form shall be filed and served at least 30 days before any scheduled hearing on the objection or any deadline for the claimant to request a hearing.
   (2) *Manner of Service*.
      (A) The objection and notice shall be served on a claimant by first-class mail to the person most recently designated on the claimant's original or amended proof of claim as the person to receive notices, at the address so indicated; and
         (i) if the objection is to a claim of the United States, or any of its officers or agencies, in the manner provided for service of a summons and complaint by Rule 7004(b)(4) or (5); or
         (ii) if the objection is to a claim of an insured depository institution, in the manner provided by Rule 7004(h).
      (B) Service of the objection and notice shall also be made by first-class mail or other permitted means on the debtor or debtor in possession, the trustee, and, if applicable, the entity filing the proof of claim under Rule 3005.

(b) **Demand for Relief Requiring an Adversary Proceeding**. A party in interest shall not include a demand for relief of a kind specified in Rule 7001 in an objection to the allowance of a claim, but may include the objection in an adversary proceeding.

(c) **Limitation on Joinder of Claims Objections**. Unless otherwise ordered by the court or permitted by subdivision (d), objections to more than one claim shall not be joined in a single objection.

(d) **Omnibus Objection**. Subject to subdivision (e), objections to more than one claim may be joined in an omnibus objection if all the claims were filed by the same entity, or the objections are based solely on the grounds that the claims should be disallowed, in whole or in part, because:

    (1) they duplicate other claims;

    (2) they have been filed in the wrong case;

    (3) they have been amended by subsequently filed proofs of claim;

    (4) they were not timely filed;

    (5) they have been satisfied or released during the case in accordance with the Code, applicable rules, or a court order;

    (6) they were presented in a form that does not comply with applicable rules, and the objection states that the objector is unable to determine the validity of the claim because of the noncompliance;

    (7) they are interests, rather than claims; or

    (8) they assert priority in an amount that exceeds the maximum amount under § 507 of the Code.

(e) **Requirements for Omnibus Objection**. An omnibus objection shall:

    (1) state in a conspicuous place that claimants receiving the objection should locate their names and claims in the objection;

    (2) list claimants alphabetically, provide a cross-reference to claim numbers, and, if appropriate, list claimants by category of claims;

    (3) state the grounds of the objection to each claim and provide a cross-reference to the pages in the omnibus objection pertinent to the stated grounds;

    (4) state in the title the identity of the objector and the grounds for the objections;

    (5) be numbered consecutively with other omnibus objections filed by the same objector; and

    (6) contain objections to no more than 100 claims.

(f) **Finality of Objection**. The finality of any order regarding a claim objection included in an omnibus objection shall be determined as though the claim had been subject to an individual objection.

Rule 3008. Reconsideration of Claims

A party in interest may move for reconsideration of an order allowing or disallowing a claim against the estate. The court after a hearing on notice shall enter an appropriate order.

Rule 3009. Declaration and Payment of Dividends in a Chapter 7 Liquidation Case

In a chapter 7 case, dividends to creditors shall be paid as promptly as practicable. Dividend checks shall be made payable to and mailed to each

62   *Rule 3010. Small Dividends and Payments in Chapter 7 Liquidation,*
Chapter 12 Family Farmer's Debt Adjustment, and Chapter 13
Individual's Debt Adjustment Cases

creditor whose claim has been allowed, unless a power of attorney authorizing another entity to receive dividends has been executed and filed in accordance with Rule 9010. In that event, dividend checks shall be made payable to the creditor and to the other entity and shall be mailed to the other entity.

Rule 3010. Small Dividends and Payments in Chapter 7 Liquidation, Chapter 12 Family Farmer's Debt Adjustment, and Chapter 13 Individual's Debt Adjustment Cases

(a) **Chapter 7 Cases**. In a chapter 7 case no dividend in an amount less than $5 shall be distributed by the trustee to any creditor unless authorized by local rule or order of the court. Any dividend not distributed to a creditor shall be treated in the same manner as unclaimed funds as provided in § 347 of the Code.

(b) **Chapter 12 and Chapter 13 Cases**. In a chapter 12 or chapter 13 case no payment in an amount less than $15 shall be distributed by the trustee to any creditor unless authorized by local rule or order of the court. Funds not distributed because of this subdivision shall accumulate and shall be paid whenever the accumulation aggregates $15. Any funds remaining shall be distributed with the final payment.

Rule 3011. Unclaimed Funds in Chapter 7 Liquidation, Chapter 12 Family Farmer's Debt Adjustment, and Chapter 13 Individual's Debt Adjustment Cases

The trustee shall file a list of all known names and addresses of the entities and the amounts which they are entitled to be paid from remaining property of the estate that is paid into court pursuant to § 347(a) of the Code.

Rule 3012. Determining the Amount of Secured and Priority Claims

(a) **Determination of Amount of Claim**. On request by a party in interest and after notice—to the holder of the claim and any other entity the court designates—and a hearing, the court may determine:

(1) the amount of a secured claim under § 506(a) of the Code; or

(2) the amount of a claim entitled to priority under § 507 of the Code.

(b) **Request for Determination; How Made**. Except as provided in subdivision (c), a request to determine the amount of a secured claim may be made by motion, in a claim objection, or in a plan filed in a chapter 12 or chapter 13 case. When the request is made in a chapter 12 or chapter 13 plan, the plan shall be served on the holder of the claim and any other entity the court designates in the manner provided for service of a summons and complaint by Rule 7004. A request to determine the amount of a claim entitled to priority may be made only by motion after a claim is filed or in a claim objection.

(c) **Claims of Governmental Units.** A request to determine the amount of a secured claim of a governmental unit may be made only by motion or in a claim objection after the governmental unit files a proof of claim or after the time for filing one under Rule 3002(c)(1) has expired.

Rule 3013. Classification of Claims and Interests

For the purposes of the plan and its acceptance, the court may, on motion after hearing on notice as the court may direct, determine classes of creditors and equity security holders pursuant to §§ 1122, 1222(b)(1), and 1322(b)(1) of the Code.

Rule 3014. Election Under Section 1111(b) by Secured Creditor in Chapter 9 Municipality or Chapter 11 Reorganization Case

An election of application of § 1111(b)(2) of the Code by a class of secured creditors in a chapter 9 or 11 case may be made at any time prior to the conclusion of the hearing on the disclosure statement or within such later time as the court may fix. If the disclosure statement is conditionally approved pursuant to Rule 3017.1, and a final hearing on the disclosure statement is not held, the election of application of § 1111(b)(2) may be made not later than the date fixed pursuant to Rule 3017.1(a)(2) or another date the court may fix. The election shall be in writing and signed unless made at the hearing on the disclosure statement. The election, if made by the majorities required by § 1111(b)(1)(A)(i), shall be binding on all members of the class with respect to the plan.

Rule 3015. Filing, Objection to Confirmation, Effect of Confirmation, and Modification of a Plan in a Chapter 12 or a Chapter 13 Case

(a) **Filing a Chapter 12 Plan.** The debtor may file a chapter 12 plan with the petition. If a plan is not filed with the petition, it shall be filed within the time prescribed by § 1221 of the Code.

(b) **Filing a Chapter 13 Plan.** The debtor may file a chapter 13 plan with the petition. If a plan is not filed with the petition, it shall be filed within 14 days thereafter, and such time may not be further extended except for cause shown and on notice as the court may direct. If a case is converted to chapter 13, a plan shall be filed within 14 days thereafter, and such time may not be further extended except for cause shown and on notice as the court may direct.

(c) **Form of Chapter 13 Plan.** If there is an Official Form for a plan filed in a chapter 13 case, that form must be used unless a Local Form has been adopted in compliance with Rule 3015.1. With either the Official Form or a Local Form, a nonstandard provision is effective only if it is included in a section of the form designated for nonstandard provisions and is also identified in accordance with any other requirements of the form. As used in this rule and the Official Form or a Local Form, "nonstandard provision" means a provision not otherwise included in the Official or Local Form or deviating from it.

(d) **Notice.** If the plan is not included with the notice of the hearing on confirmation mailed under Rule 2002 , the debtor shall serve the plan on the trustee and all creditors when it is filed with the court.

(e) **Transmission to United States Trustee.** The clerk shall forthwith transmit to the United States trustee a copy of the plan and any modification thereof filed under subdivision (a) or (b) of this rule.

(f) **Objection to Confirmation; Determination of Good Faith in the Absence of an Objection.** An objection to confirmation of a plan shall be filed and served on the debtor, the trustee, and any other entity designated by the court, and shall be transmitted to the United States trustee at least seven days before the date set for the hearing on confirmation, unless the court orders otherwise. An objection to confirmation is governed by Rule 9014. If no objection is timely filed, the court may determine that the plan has been proposed in good faith and not by any means forbidden by law without receiving evidence on such issues.

(g) **Effect of Confirmation.** Upon the confirmation of a chapter 12 or chapter 13 plan:

   (1) any determination in the plan made under Rule 3012 about the amount of a secured claim is binding on the holder of the claim, even if the holder files a contrary proof of claim or the debtor schedules that claim, and regardless of whether an objection to the claim has been filed; and

   (2) any request in the plan to terminate the stay imposed by § 362(a), § 1201(a), or § 1301(a) is granted.

(h) **Modification of Plan After Confirmation.** A request to modify a plan under § 1229 or § 1329 of the Code shall identify the proponent and shall be filed together with the proposed modification. The clerk, or some other person as the court may direct, shall give the debtor, the trustee, and all creditors not less than 21 days notice by mail of the time fixed for filing objections and, if an objection is filed, the hearing to consider the proposed modification, unless the court orders otherwise with respect to creditors who are not affected by the proposed modification. A copy of the notice shall be transmitted to the United States trustee. A copy of the proposed modification, or a summary thereof, shall be included with the notice. Any objection to the proposed modification shall be filed and served on the debtor, the trustee, and any other entity designated by the court, and shall be transmitted to the United States trustee. An objection to a proposed modification is governed by Rule 9014.

Rule 3015.1. Requirements for a Local Form for Plans Filed in a Chapter 13 Case

Notwithstanding Rule 9029(a)(1), a district may require that a Local Form for a plan filed in a chapter 13 case be used instead of an Official Form adopted for that purpose if the following conditions are satisfied:

(a) a single Local Form is adopted for the district after public notice and an opportunity for public comment;

(b) each paragraph is numbered and labeled in boldface type with a heading stating the general subject matter of the paragraph;

(c) the Local Form includes an initial paragraph for the debtor to indicate that the plan does or does not:

    (1) contain any nonstandard provision;

    (2) limit the amount of a secured claim based on a valuation of the collateral for the claim; or

    (3) avoid a security interest or lien;

(d) the Local Form contains separate paragraphs for:

    (1) curing any default and maintaining payments on a claim secured by the debtor's principal residence;

    (2) paying a domestic-support obligation;

    (3) paying a claim described in the final paragraph of § 1325(a) of the Bankruptcy Code; and

    (4) surrendering property that secures a claim with a request that the stay under §§ 362(a) and 1301(a) be terminated as to the surrendered collateral; and

(e) the Local Form contains a final paragraph for:

    (1) the placement of nonstandard provisions, as defined in Rule 3015(c), along with a statement that any nonstandard provision placed elsewhere in the plan is void; and

    (2) certification by the debtor's attorney or by an unrepresented debtor that the plan contains no nonstandard provision other than those set out in the final paragraph.

Rule 3016. Filing of Plan and Disclosure Statement in a Chapter 9 Municipality or Chapter 11 Reorganization Case

(a) **Identification of Plan.** Every proposed plan and any modification thereof shall be dated and, in a chapter 11 case, identified with the name of the entity or entities submitting or filing it.

(b) **Disclosure Statement.** In a chapter 9 or 11 case, a disclosure statement under § 1125 of the Code or evidence showing compliance with § 1126(b) shall be filed with the plan or within a time fixed by the court, unless the plan is intended to provide adequate information under § 1125(f)(1). If the plan is intended to provide adequate information under § 1125(f)(1), it shall be so designated and Rule 3017.1 shall apply as if the plan is a disclosure statement.

(c) **Injunction Under a Plan.** If a plan provides for an injunction against conduct not otherwise enjoined under the Code, the plan and disclosure statement shall describe in specific and conspicuous language (bold, italic, or underlined text) all acts to be enjoined and identify the entities that would be subject to the injunction.

(d) **Standard Form Small Business Disclosure Statement and Plan.** In a small business case, the court may approve a disclosure statement and may confirm a plan that conform substantially to the appropriate Official Forms or other standard forms approved by the court.

Rule 3017. Court Consideration of Disclosure Statement in a Chapter 9 Municipality or Chapter 11 Reorganization Case

(a) **Hearing on Disclosure Statement and Objections.** Except as provided in Rule 3017.1, after a disclosure statement is filed in accordance with Rule 3016(b), the court shall hold a hearing on at least 28 days' notice to the debtor, creditors, equity security holders and other parties in interest as provided in Rule 2002 to consider the disclosure statement and any objections or modifications thereto. The plan and the disclosure statement shall be mailed with the notice of the hearing only to the debtor, any trustee or committee appointed under the Code, the Securities and Exchange Commission and any party in interest who requests in writing a copy of the statement or plan. Objections to the disclosure statement shall be filed and served on the debtor, the trustee, any committee appointed under the Code, and any other entity designated by the court, at any time before the disclosure statement is approved or by an earlier date as the court may fix. In a chapter 11 reorganization case, every notice, plan, disclosure statement, and objection required to be served or mailed pursuant to this subdivision shall be transmitted to the United States trustee within the time provided in this subdivision.

(b) **Determination on Disclosure Statement.** Following the hearing the court shall determine whether the disclosure statement should be approved.

(c) **Dates Fixed for Voting on Plan and Confirmation.** On or before approval of the disclosure statement, the court shall fix a time within which the holders of claims and interests may accept or reject the plan and may fix a date for the hearing on confirmation.

(d) **Transmission and Notice to United States Trustee, Creditors, and Equity Security Holders.** Upon approval of a disclosure statement, — except to the extent that the court orders otherwise with respect to one or more unimpaired classes of creditors or equity security holders—the debtor in possession, trustee, proponent of the plan, or clerk as the court orders shall mail to all creditors and equity security holders, and in a chapter 11 reorganization case shall transmit to the United States trustee,

(1) the plan or a court-approved summary of the plan;
(2) the disclosure statement approved by the court;
(3) notice of the time within which acceptances and rejections of the plan may be filed; and
(4) any other information as the court may direct, including any court opinion approving the disclosure statement or a court-approved summary of the opinion.

In addition, notice of the time fixed for filing objections and the hearing on confirmation shall be mailed to all creditors and equity security holders in accordance with Rule 2002(b), and a form of ballot conforming to the appropriate Official Form shall be mailed to creditors and equity security holders entitled to vote on the plan. If the court opinion is not transmitted or only a summary of the plan is transmitted, the court opinion or the plan shall be provided on request of a party in interest at the plan proponent's expense. If the court orders that the disclosure statement and the plan or a summary of the plan shall not be mailed to any unimpaired class, notice that the class is designated in the plan as unimpaired and notice of the name and address of the person from whom the plan or summary of the plan and disclosure statement may be obtained upon request and at the plan proponent's expense, shall be mailed to members of the unimpaired class together with the notice of the time fixed for filing objections to and the hearing on confirmation. For the purposes of this subdivision, creditors and equity security holders shall include holders of stock, bonds, debentures, notes, and other securities of record on the date the order approving the disclosure statement is entered or another date fixed by the court, for cause, after notice and a hearing.

(e) Transmission to Beneficial Holders of Securities. At the hearing held pursuant to subdivision (a) of this rule the court shall consider the procedures for transmitting the documents and information required by subdivision (d) of this rule to beneficial holders of stock, bonds, debentures, notes and other securities, determine the adequacy of the procedures, and enter any orders the court deems appropriate.

(f) Notice and Transmission of Documents to Entities Subject to an Injunction Under a Plan. If a plan provides for an injunction against conduct not otherwise enjoined under the Code and an entity that would be subject to the injunction is not a creditor or equity security holder, at the hearing held under Rule 3017(a), the court shall consider procedures for providing the entity with:

(1) at least 28 days' notice of the time fixed for filing objections and the hearing on confirmation of the plan containing the information described in Rule 2002(c)(3); and
(2) to the extent feasible, a copy of the plan and disclosure statement.

Rule 3017.1. Court Consideration of Disclosure Statement in a Small Business Case

(a) **Conditional Approval of Disclosure Statement.** In a small business case, the court may, on application of the plan proponent or on its own initiative, conditionally approve a disclosure statement filed in accordance with Rule 3016. On or before conditional approval of the disclosure statement, the court shall:

    (1) fix a time within which the holders of claims and interests may accept or reject the plan;

    (2) fix a time for filing objections to the disclosure statement;

    (3) fix a date for the hearing on final approval of the disclosure statement to be held if a timely objection is filed; and

    (4) fix a date for the hearing on confirmation.

(b) **Application of Rule 3017.** Rule 3017(a), (b), (c), and (e) do not apply to a conditionally approved disclosure statement. Rule 3017(d) applies to a conditionally approved disclosure statement, except that conditional approval is considered approval of the disclosure statement for the purpose of applying Rule 3017(d).

(c) **Final Approval.**

    (1) *Notice.* Notice of the time fixed for filing objections and the hearing to consider final approval of the disclosure statement shall be given in accordance with Rule 2002 and may be combined with notice of the hearing on confirmation of the plan.

    (2) *Objections.* Objections to the disclosure statement shall be filed, transmitted to the United States trustee, and served on the debtor, the trustee, any committee appointed under the Code and any other entity designated by the court at any time before final approval of the disclosure statement or by an earlier date as the court may fix.

    (3) *Hearing.* If a timely objection to the disclosure statement is filed, the court shall hold a hearing to consider final approval before or combined with the hearing on confirmation of the plan.

Rule 3018. Acceptance or Rejection of Plan in a Chapter 9 Municipality or a Chapter 11 Reorganization Case

(a) **Entities Entitled to Accept or Reject Plan; Time for Acceptance or Rejection.** A plan may be accepted or rejected in accordance with § 1126 of the Code within the time fixed by the court pursuant to Rule 3017. Subject to subdivision (b) of this rule, an equity security holder or creditor whose claim is based on a security of record shall not be entitled to accept or reject a plan unless the equity security holder or creditor is the holder of record of the security on the date the order approving the disclosure statement is entered or on another date fixed by the court, for cause, after notice and a hearing. For cause shown, the court after notice and hearing may permit a creditor or equity security holder to change or withdraw an acceptance or rejection. Notwithstanding objection to a claim or interest, the court after notice and hearing may temporarily allow the claim or interest in an amount which the court deems proper for the purpose of accepting or rejecting a plan.

(b) **Acceptances or Rejections Obtained Before Petition.** An equity security holder or creditor whose claim is based on a security of record who accepted or rejected the plan before the commencement of the case shall not be deemed to have accepted or rejected the plan pursuant to § 1126(b) of the Code unless the equity security holder or creditor was the holder of record of the security on the date specified in the solicitation of such acceptance or rejection for the purposes of such solicitation. A holder of a claim or interest who has accepted or rejected a plan before the commencement of the case under the Code shall not be deemed to have accepted or rejected the plan if the court finds after notice and hearing that the plan was not transmitted to substantially all creditors and equity security holders of the same class, that an unreasonably short time was prescribed for such creditors and equity security holders to accept or reject the plan, or that the solicitation was not in compliance with § 1126(b) of the Code.

(c) **Form of Acceptance or Rejection.** An acceptance or rejection shall be in writing, identify the plan or plans accepted or rejected, be signed by the creditor or equity security holder or an authorized agent, and conform to the appropriate Official Form. If more than one plan is transmitted pursuant to Rule 3017, an acceptance or rejection may be filed by each creditor or equity security holder for any number of plans transmitted and if acceptances are filed for more than one plan, the creditor or equity security holder may indicate a preference or preferences among the plans so accepted.

(d) **Acceptance or Rejection by Partially Secured Creditor.** A creditor whose claim has been allowed in part as a secured claim and in part as an unsecured claim shall be entitled to accept or reject a plan in both capacities.

Rule 3019. Modification of Accepted Plan in a Chapter 9 Municipality or a Chapter 11 Reorganization Case

(a) Modification of Plan Before Confirmation. In a chapter 9 or chapter 11 case, after a plan has been accepted and before its confirmation, the proponent may file a modification of the plan. If the court finds after hearing on notice to the trustee, any committee appointed under the Code, and any other entity designated by the court that the proposed modification does not adversely change the treatment of the claim of any creditor or the interest of any equity security holder who has not accepted in writing the modification, it shall be deemed accepted by all creditors and equity security holders who have previously accepted the plan.

(b) Modification of Plan After Confirmation in Individual Debtor Case. If the debtor is an individual, a request to modify the plan under § 1127(e) of the

Code is governed by Rule 9014. The request shall identify the proponent and shall be filed together with the proposed modification. The clerk, or some other person as the court may direct, shall give the debtor, the trustee, and all creditors not less than 21 days' notice by mail of the time fixed to file objections and, if an objection is filed, the hearing to consider the proposed modification, unless the court orders otherwise with respect to creditors who are not affected by the proposed modification. A copy of the notice shall be transmitted to the United States trustee, together with a copy of the proposed modification. Any objection to the proposed modification shall be filed and served on the debtor, the proponent of the modification, the trustee, and any other entity designated by the court, and shall be transmitted to the United States trustee.

Rule 3020. Deposit; Confirmation of Plan in a Chapter 9 Municipality or Chapter 11 Reorganization Case

(a) **Deposit**. In a chapter 11 case, prior to entry of the order confirming the plan, the court may order the deposit with the trustee or debtor in possession of the consideration required by the plan to be distributed on confirmation. Any money deposited shall be kept in a special account established for the exclusive purpose of making the distribution.

(b) **Objection to and Hearing on Confirmation in a Chapter 9 or Chapter 11 Case**.

  (1) *Objection*. An objection to confirmation of the plan shall be filed and served on the debtor, the trustee, the proponent of the plan, any committee appointed under the Code, and any other entity designated by the court, within a time fixed by the court. Unless the case is a chapter 9 municipality case, a copy of every objection to confirmation shall be transmitted by the objecting party to the United States trustee within the time fixed for filing objections. An objection to confirmation is governed by Rule 9014.

  (2) *Hearing*. The court shall rule on confirmation of the plan after notice and hearing as provided in Rule 2002. If no objection is timely filed, the court may determine that the plan has been proposed in good faith and not by any means forbidden by law without receiving evidence on such issues.

(c) **Order of Confirmation**.

  (1) The order of confirmation shall conform to the appropriate Official Form. If the plan provides for an injunction against conduct not otherwise enjoined under the Code, the order of confirmation shall (1) describe in reasonable detail all acts enjoined; (2) be specific in its terms regarding the injunction; and (3) identify the entities subject to the injunction.

  (2) Notice of entry of the order of confirmation shall be mailed promptly to the debtor, the trustee, creditors, equity security holders, other parties in interest, and, if known, to any identified entity subject to an

injunction provided for in the plan against conduct not otherwise enjoined under the Code.

(3) Except in a chapter 9 municipality case, notice of entry of the order of confirmation shall be transmitted to the United States trustee as provided in Rule 2002(k).

(d) **Retained Power.** Notwithstanding the entry of the order of confirmation, the court may issue any other order necessary to administer the estate.

(e) **Stay of Confirmation Order.** An order confirming a plan is stayed until the expiration of 14 days after the entry of the order, unless the court orders otherwise.

Rule 3021. Distribution Under Plan

Except as provided in Rule 3020(e), after a plan is confirmed, distribution shall be made to creditors whose claims have been allowed, to interest holders whose interests have not been disallowed, and to indenture trustees who have filed claims under Rule 3003(c)(5) that have been allowed. For purposes of this rule, creditors include holders of bonds, debentures, notes, and other debt securities, and interest holders include the holders of stock and other equity securities, of record at the time of commencement of distribution, unless a different time is fixed by the plan or the order confirming the plan.

Rule 3022. Final Decree in Chapter 11 Reorganization Case

After an estate is fully administered in a chapter 11 reorganization case, the court, on its own motion or on motion of a party in interest, shall enter a final decree closing the case.

Part IV. The debtor: duties and benefits

Rule 4001. Relief from Automatic Stay; Prohibiting or Conditioning the Use, Sale, or Lease of Property; Use of Cash Collateral; Obtaining Credit; Agreements

(a) **Relief from Stay; Prohibiting or Conditioning the Use, Sale, or Lease of Property.**

    (1) *Motion.* A motion for relief from an automatic stay provided by the Code or a motion to prohibit or condition the use, sale, or lease of property pursuant to § 363(e) shall be made in accordance with Rule 9014 and shall be served on any committee elected pursuant to § 705 or appointed pursuant to § 1102 of the Code or its authorized agent, or, if the case is a chapter 9 municipality case or a chapter 11 reorganization case and no committee of unsecured creditors has been appointed pursuant to § 1102, on the creditors included on the list filed pursuant to Rule 1007(d), and on such other entities as the court may direct.

    (2) *Ex Parte Relief.* Relief from a stay under § 362(a) or a request to prohibit or condition the use, sale, or lease of property pursuant to § 363(e) may be granted without prior notice only if (A) it clearly appears from specific facts shown by affidavit or by a verified motion that immediate and irreparable injury, loss, or damage will result to the movant before the adverse party or the attorney for the adverse party can be heard in opposition, and (B) the movant's attorney certifies to the court in writing the efforts, if any, which have been made to give notice and the reasons why notice should not be required. The party obtaining relief under this subdivision and § 362(f) or § 363(e) shall immediately give oral notice thereof to the trustee or debtor in possession and to the debtor and forthwith mail or otherwise transmit to such adverse party or parties a copy of the order granting relief. On two days notice to the party who obtained relief from the stay without notice or on shorter notice to that party as the court may prescribe, the adverse party may appear and move reinstatement of the stay or reconsideration of the order prohibiting or conditioning the use, sale, or lease of property. In that event, the court shall proceed expeditiously to hear and determine the motion.

    (3) *Stay of Order.* An order granting a motion for relief from an automatic stay made in accordance with Rule 4001(a)(1) is stayed until the expiration of 14 days after the entry of the order, unless the court orders otherwise.

(b) **Use of Cash Collateral.**

    (1) *Motion; Service.*

        (A) Motion. A motion for authority to use cash collateral shall be made in accordance with Rule 9014 and shall be accompanied by a proposed form of order.

(B) Contents. The motion shall consist of or (if the motion is more than five pages in length) begin with a concise statement of the relief requested, not to exceed five pages, that lists or summarizes, and sets out the location within the relevant documents of, all material provisions, including:
  (i)   the name of each entity with an interest in the cash collateral;
  (ii) the purposes for the use of the cash collateral;
  (iii) the material terms, including duration, of the use of the cash collateral; and
  (iv) any liens, cash payments, or other adequate protection that will be provided to each entity with an interest in the cash collateral or, if no additional adequate protection is proposed, an explanation of why each entity's interest is adequately protected. (C) Service. The motion shall be served on: (1) any entity with an interest in the cash collateral; (2) any committee elected under § 705 or appointed under § 1102 of the Code, or its authorized agent, or, if the case is a chapter 9 municipality case or a chapter 11 reorganization case and no committee of unsecured creditors has been appointed under § 1102, the creditors included on the list filed under Rule 1007(d); and (3) any other entity that the court directs.

(2) *Hearing.* The court may commence a final hearing on a motion for authorization to use cash collateral no earlier than 14 days after service of the motion. If the motion so requests, the court may conduct a preliminary hearing before such 14 day period expires, but the court may authorize the use of only that amount of cash collateral as is necessary to avoid immediate and irreparable harm to the estate pending a final hearing.

(3) *Notice.* Notice of hearing pursuant to this subdivision shall be given to the parties on whom service of the motion is required by paragraph (1) of this subdivision and to such other entities as the court may direct.

(c) **Obtaining Credit.**
  (1) *Motion; Service.*
    (A) Motion. A motion for authority to obtain credit shall be made in accordance with Rule 9014 and shall be accompanied by a copy of the credit agreement and a proposed form of order.
    (B) Contents. The motion shall consist of or (if the motion is more than five pages in length) begin with a concise statement of the relief requested, not to exceed five pages, that lists or summarizes, and sets out the location within the relevant documents of, all material provisions of the proposed credit agreement and form of order, including interest rate, maturity,

events of default, liens, borrowing limits, and borrowing conditions. If the proposed credit agreement or form of order includes any of the provisions listed below, the concise statement shall also: briefly list or summarize each one; identify its specific location in the proposed agreement and form of order; and identify any such provision that is proposed to remain in effect if interim approval is granted, but final relief is denied, as provided under Rule 4001(c)(2). In addition, the motion shall describe the nature and extent of each provision listed below:

(i) a grant of priority or a lien on property of the estate under § 364(c) or (d);

(ii) the providing of adequate protection or priority for a claim that arose before the commencement of the case, including the granting of a lien on property of the estate to secure the claim, or the use of property of the estate or credit obtained under § 364 to make cash payments on account of the claim;

(iii) a determination of the validity, enforceability, priority, or amount of a claim that arose before the commencement of the case, or of any lien securing the claim;

(iv) a waiver or modification of Code provisions or applicable rules relating to the automatic stay;

(v) a waiver or modification of any entity's authority or right to file a plan, seek an extension of time in which the debtor has the exclusive right to file a plan, request the use of cash collateral under § 363(c), or request authority to obtain credit under § 364;

(vi) the establishment of deadlines for filing a plan of reorganization, for approval of a disclosure statement, for a hearing on confirmation, or for entry of a confirmation order;

(vii) a waiver or modification of the applicability of nonbankruptcy law relating to the perfection of a lien on property of the estate, or on the foreclosure or other enforcement of the lien;

(viii) a release, waiver, or limitation on any claim or other cause of action belonging to the estate or the trustee, including any modification of the statute of limitations or other deadline to commence an action;

(ix) the indemnification of any entity;

(x) a release, waiver, or limitation of any right under § 506(c); or

(xi) the granting of a lien on any claim or cause of action arising under §§ 544, 545, 547, 548, 549, 553(b), 723(a), or 724(a).

(C) Service. The motion shall be served on: (1) any committee elected under § 705 or appointed under § 1102 of the Code, or its authorized agent, or, if the case is a chapter 9 municipality case

76   *Rule 4001. Relief from Automatic Stay; Prohibiting or Conditioning the
Use, Sale, or Lease of Property; Use of Cash Collateral; Obtaining Credit;
Agreements*

or a chapter 11 reorganization case and no committee of
unsecured creditors has been appointed under § 1102, on the
creditors included on the list filed under Rule 1007(d); and (2) on
any other entity that the court directs.

(2) *Hearing.* The court may commence a final hearing on a motion for
authority to obtain credit no earlier than 14 days after service of the
motion. If the motion so requests, the court may conduct a hearing
before such 14 day period expires, but the court may authorize the
obtaining of credit only to the extent necessary to avoid immediate
and irreparable harm to the estate pending a final hearing.

(3) Notice. Notice of hearing pursuant to this subdivision shall be given
to the parties on whom service of the motion is required by paragraph
(1) of this subdivision and to such other entities as the court may
direct.

(d) **Agreement Relating to Relief from the Automatic Stay, Prohibiting or
Conditioning the Use, Sale, or Lease of Property, Providing Adequate
Protection, Use of Cash Collateral, and Obtaining Credit.**

(1) *Motion; Service.*

(A) Motion. A motion for approval of any of the following shall be
accompanied by a copy of the agreement and a proposed form of
order:

(i)   an agreement to provide adequate protection;

(ii) an agreement to prohibit or condition the use, sale, or lease
of property;

(iii) an agreement to modify or terminate the stay provided for in
§ 362;

(iv) an agreement to use cash collateral; or

(v)   an agreement between the debtor and an entity that has a lien
or interest in property of the estate pursuant to which the
entity consents to the creation of a lien senior or equal to the
entity's lien or interest in such property.

(B) Contents. The motion shall consist of or (if the motion is more
than five pages in length) begin with a concise statement of the
relief requested, not to exceed five pages, that lists or
summarizes, and sets out the location within the relevant
documents of, all material provisions of the agreement. In
addition, the concise statement shall briefly list or summarize,
and identify the specific location of, each provision in the
proposed form of order, agreement, or other document of the
type listed in subdivision (c)(1)(B). The motion shall also
describe the nature and extent of each such provision.

(C) Service. The motion shall be served on: (1) any committee
elected under § 705 or appointed under § 1102 of the Code, or its
authorized agent, or, if the case is a chapter 9 municipality case
or a chapter 11 reorganization case and no committee of

unsecured creditors has been appointed under § 1102, on the creditors included on the list filed under Rule 1007(d); and (2) on any other entity the court directs.

(2) *Objection.* Notice of the motion and the time within which objections may be filed and served on the debtor in possession or trustee shall be mailed to the parties on whom service is required by paragraph (1) of this subdivision and to such other entities as the court may direct. Unless the court fixes a different time, objections may be filed within 14 days of the mailing of the notice.

(3) *Disposition; Hearing.* If no objection is filed, the court may enter an order approving or disapproving the agreement without conducting a hearing. If an objection is filed or if the court determines a hearing is appropriate, the court shall hold a hearing on no less than seven days' notice to the objector, the movant, the parties on whom service is required by paragraph (1) of this subdivision and such other entities as the court may direct.

(4) *Agreement in Settlement of Motion.* The court may direct that the procedures prescribed in paragraphs (1), (2), and (3) of this subdivision shall not apply and the agreement may be approved without further notice if the court determines that a motion made pursuant to subdivisions (a), (b), or (c) of this rule was sufficient to afford reasonable notice of the material provisions of the agreement and opportunity for a hearing.

Rule 4002. Duties of Debtor

(a) **In General.** In addition to performing other duties prescribed by the Code and rules, the debtor shall:

(1) attend and submit to an examination at the times ordered by the court;

(2) attend the hearing on a complaint objecting to discharge and testify, if called as a witness;

(3) inform the trustee immediately in writing as to the location of real property in which the debtor has an interest and the name and address of every person holding money or property subject to the debtor's withdrawal or order if a schedule of property has not yet been filed pursuant to Rule 1007;

(4) cooperate with the trustee in the preparation of an inventory, the examination of proofs of claim, and the administration of the estate; and

(5) file a statement of any change of the debtor's address.

(b) **Individual Debtor's Duty to Provide Documentation.**

(1) *Personal Identification.* Every individual debtor shall bring to the meeting of creditors under § 341:

(A) a picture identification issued by a governmental unit, or other personal identifying information that establishes the debtor's identity; and

    (B) evidence of social-security number(s), or a written statement that such documentation does not exist.

(2) *Financial Information.* Every individual debtor shall bring to the meeting of creditors under § 341, and make available to the trustee, the following documents or copies of them, or provide a written statement that the documentation does not exist or is not in the debtor's possession:

    (A) evidence of current income such as the most recent payment advice;

    (B) unless the trustee or the United States trustee instructs otherwise, statements for each of the debtor's depository and investment accounts, including checking, savings, and money market accounts, mutual funds and brokerage accounts for the time period that includes the date of the filing of the petition; and

    (C) documentation of monthly expenses claimed by the debtor if required by § 707(b)(2)(A) or (B).

(3) *Tax Return.* At least 7 days before the first date set for the meeting of creditors under § 341, the debtor shall provide to the trustee a copy of the debtor's federal income tax return for the most recent tax year ending immediately before the commencement of the case and for which a return was filed, including any attachments, or a transcript of the tax return, or provide a written statement that the documentation does not exist.

(4) *Tax Returns Provided to Creditors.* If a creditor, at least 14 days before the first date set for the meeting of creditors under § 341, requests a copy of the debtor's tax return that is to be provided to the trustee under subdivision (b)(3), the debtor, at least 7 days before the first date set for the meeting of creditors under § 341, shall provide to the requesting creditor a copy of the return, including any attachments, or a transcript of the tax return, or provide a written statement that the documentation does not exist.

(5) *Confidentiality of Tax Information.* The debtor's obligation to provide tax returns under Rule 4002(b)(3) and (b)(4) is subject to procedures for safeguarding the confidentiality of tax information established by the Director of the Administrative Office of the United States Courts.

Rule 4003. Exemptions

(a) **Claim of Exemptions**. A debtor shall list the property claimed as exempt under § 522 of the Code on the schedule of assets required to be filed by Rule 1007. If the debtor fails to claim exemptions or file the schedule within the time specified in Rule 1007, a dependent of the debtor may file the list within 30 days thereafter.

(b) **Objecting to a Claim of Exemptions**.

    (1) Except as provided in paragraphs (2) and (3), a party in interest may file an objection to the list of property claimed as exempt within 30 days after the meeting of creditors held under § 341(a) is concluded

or within 30 days after any amendment to the list or supplemental schedules is filed, whichever is later. The court may, for cause, extend the time for filing objections if, before the time to object expires, a party in interest files a request for an extension.

(2) The trustee may file an objection to a claim of exemption at any time prior to one year after the closing of the case if the debtor fraudulently asserted the claim of exemption. The trustee shall deliver or mail the objection to the debtor and the debtor's attorney, and to any person filing the list of exempt property and that person's attorney.

(3) An objection to a claim of exemption based on § 522(q) shall be filed before the closing of the case. If an exemption is first claimed after a case is reopened, an objection shall be filed before the reopened case is closed.

(4) A copy of any objection shall be delivered or mailed to the trustee, the debtor and the debtor's attorney, and the person filing the list and that person's attorney.

(c) **Burden of Proof**. In any hearing under this rule, the objecting party has the burden of proving that the exemptions are not properly claimed. After hearing on notice, the court shall determine the issues presented by the objections.

(d) **Avoidance by Debtor of Transfers of Exempt Property**. A proceeding under § 522(f) to avoid a lien or other transfer of property exempt under of the Code shall be commenced by motion in the manner provided by Rule 9014, or by serving a chapter 12 or chapter 13 plan on the affected creditors in the manner provided by Rule 7004 for service of a summons and complaint. Notwithstanding the provisions of subdivision (b), a creditor may object to a request under § 522(f) by challenging the validity of the exemption asserted to be impaired by the lien.

Rule 4004. Grant or Denial of Discharge

(a) **Time for Objecting to Discharge; Notice of Time Fixed**. In a chapter 7 case, a complaint, or a motion under § 727(a)(8) or (a)(9) of the Code, objecting to the debtor's discharge shall be filed no later than 60 days after the first date set for the meeting of creditors under § 341(a). In a chapter 11 case, the complaint shall be filed no later than the first date set for the hearing on confirmation. In a chapter 13 case, a motion objecting to the debtor's discharge under § 1328(f) shall be filed no later than 60 days after the first date set for the meeting of creditors under § 341(a). At least 28 days' notice of the time so fixed shall be given to the United States trustee and all creditors as provided in Rule 2002(f) and (k) and to the trustee and the trustee's attorney.

(b) **Extension of Time**.

(1) On motion of any party in interest, after notice and hearing, the court may for cause extend the time to object to discharge. Except as

provided in subdivision (b)(2), the motion shall be filed before the time has expired.

(2) A motion to extend the time to object to discharge may be filed after the time for objection has expired and before discharge is granted if (A) the objection is based on facts that, if learned after the discharge, would provide a basis for revocation under § 727(d) of the Code, and (B) the movant did not have knowledge of those facts in time to permit an objection. The motion shall be filed promptly after the movant discovers the facts on which the objection is based.

(c) **Grant of Discharge.**

(1) In a chapter 7 case, on expiration of the times fixed for objecting to discharge and for filing a motion to dismiss the case under Rule 1017(e), the court shall forthwith grant the discharge, except that the court shall not grant the discharge if:

(A) the debtor is not an individual;

(B) a complaint, or a motion under § 727(a)(8) or (a)(9), objecting to the discharge has been filed and not decided in the debtor's favor;

(C) the debtor has filed a waiver under § 727(a)(10);

(D) a motion to dismiss the case under § 707 is pending;

(E) a motion to extend the time for filing a complaint objecting to the discharge is pending;

(F) a motion to extend the time for filing a motion to dismiss the case under Rule 1017(e)(1) is pending;

(G) the debtor has not paid in full the filing fee prescribed by 28 U.S.C. § 1930(a) and any other fee prescribed by the Judicial Conference of the United States under 28 U.S.C. § 1930(b) that is payable to the clerk upon the commencement of a case under the Code, unless the court has waived the fees under 28 U.S.C. § 1930(f);

(H) the debtor has not filed with the court a statement of completion of a course concerning personal financial management if required by Rule 1007(b)(7);

(I) a motion to delay or postpone discharge under § 727(a)(12) is pending;

(J) a motion to enlarge the time to file a reaffirmation agreement under Rule 4008(a) is pending;

(K) a presumption is in effect under § 524(m) that a reaffirmation agreement is an undue hardship and the court has not concluded a hearing on the presumption; or

(L) a motion is pending to delay discharge, because the debtor has not filed with the court all tax documents required to be filed under § 521(f).

(2) Notwithstanding Rule 4004(c)(1), on motion of the debtor, the court may defer the entry of an order granting a discharge for 30 days and, on motion within that period, the court may defer entry of the order to a date certain.

(3) If the debtor is required to file a statement under Rule 1007(b)(8), the court shall not grant a discharge earlier than 30 days after the statement is filed.

(4) In a chapter 11 case in which the debtor is an individual, or a chapter 13 case, the court shall not grant a discharge if the debtor has not filed any statement required by Rule 1007(b)(7).

(d) **Applicability of Rules in Part VII and Rule 9014.** An objection to discharge is governed by Part VII of these rules, except that an objection to discharge under § 727(a)(8), (a)(9), or 1328(f) is commenced by motion and governed by Rule 9014.

(e) **Order of Discharge.** An order of discharge shall conform to the appropriate Official Form.

(f) **Registration in Other Districts.** An order of discharge that has become final may be registered in any other district by filing a certified copy of the order in the office of the clerk of that district. When so registered the order of discharge shall have the same effect as an order of the court of the district where registered.

(g) **Notice of Discharge.** The clerk shall promptly mail a copy of the final order of discharge to those specified in subdivision (a) of this rule.

Rule 4005. Burden of Proof in Objecting to Discharge

At the trial on a complaint objecting to a discharge, the plaintiff has the burden of proving the objection.

Rule 4006. Notice of No Discharge

If an order is entered: denying a discharge; revoking a discharge; approving a waiver of discharge; or, in the case of an individual debtor, closing the case without the entry of a discharge, the clerk shall promptly notify all parties in interest in the manner provided by Rule 2002.

Rule 4007. Determination of Dischargeability of a Debt

(a) **Persons Entitled to File Complaint.** A debtor or any creditor may file a complaint to obtain a determination of the dischargeability of any debt.

(b) **Time for Commencing Proceeding Other Than Under § 523(c) of the Code.** A complaint other than under § 523(c) may be filed at any time. A case may be reopened without payment of an additional filing fee for the purpose of filing a complaint to obtain a determination under this rule.

(c) **Time for Filing Complaint Under § 523(c) in a Chapter 7 Liquidation, Chapter 11 Reorganization, Chapter 12 Family Farmer's Debt Adjustment Case, or Chapter 13 Individual's Debt Adjustment Case; Notice of Time Fixed.** Except as otherwise provided in subdivision (d), a complaint to determine the dischargeability of a debt under § 523(c) shall be filed no later than 60 days after the first date set for the meeting of creditors under § 341(a). The court shall give all creditors no less than 30 days' notice of the time so fixed in the manner provided in Rule 2002. On motion of a party in interest, after hearing on notice, the court may for cause extend the time fixed under this subdivision. The motion shall be filed before the time has expired.

(d) **Time for Filing Complaint Under § 523(a)(6) in a Chapter 13 Individual's Debt Adjustment Case; Notice of Time Fixed.** On motion by a debtor for a discharge under § 1328(b), the court shall enter an order fixing the time to file a complaint to determine the dischargeability of any debt under § 523(a)(6) and shall give no less than 30 days' notice of the time fixed to all creditors in the manner provided in Rule 2002. On motion of any party in interest, after hearing on notice, the court may for cause extend the time fixed under this subdivision. The motion shall be filed before the time has expired.

(e) **Applicability of Rules in Part VII.** A proceeding commenced by a complaint filed under this rule is governed by Part VII of these rules.

Rule 4008. Filing of Reaffirmation Agreement; Statement in Support of Reaffirmation Agreement

(a) **Filing of Reaffirmation Agreement.** A reaffirmation agreement shall be filed no later than 60 days after the first date set for the meeting of creditors under § 341(a) of the Code. The reaffirmation agreement shall be accompanied by a cover sheet, prepared as prescribed by the appropriate Official Form. The court may, at any time and in its discretion, enlarge the time to file a reaffirmation agreement.

(b) **Statement in Support of Reaffirmation Agreement.** The debtor's statement required under § 524(k)(6)(A) of the Code shall be accompanied by a statement of the total income and expenses stated on schedules I and J. If there is a difference between the total income and expenses stated on those schedules and the statement required under § 524(k)(6)(A), the statement required by this subdivision shall include an explanation of the difference.

Part V. Courts and clerks

Rule 5001. Courts and Clerks' Offices

(a) **Courts Always Open**. The courts shall be deemed always open for the purpose of filing any pleading or other proper paper, issuing and returning process, and filing, making, or entering motions, orders and rules.

(b) **Trials and Hearings; Orders in Chambers**. All trials and hearings shall be conducted in open court and so far as convenient in a regular court room. Except as otherwise provided in 152(c), all other acts or proceedings may be done or conducted by a judge in chambers and at any place either within or without the district; but no hearing, other than one ex parte, shall be conducted outside the district without the consent of all parties affected thereby.

(c) **Clerk's Office**. The clerk's office with the clerk or a deputy in attendance shall be open during business hours on all days except Saturdays, Sundays and the legal holidays listed in Rule 9006(a).

Rule 5002. Restrictions on Approval of Appointments

(a) **Approval of Appointment of Relatives Prohibited**. The appointment of an individual as a trustee or examiner pursuant to § 1104 of the Code shall not be approved by the court if the individual is a relative of the bankruptcy judge approving the appointment or the United States trustee in the region in which the case is pending. The employment of an individual as an attorney, accountant, appraiser, auctioneer, or other professional person pursuant to §§ 327, 1103, or 1114 shall not be approved by the court if the individual is a relative of the bankruptcy judge approving the employment. The employment of an individual as attorney, accountant, appraiser, auctioneer, or other professional person pursuant to §§ 327, 1103, or 1114 may be approved by the court if the individual is a relative of the United States trustee in the region in which the case is pending, unless the court finds that the relationship with the United States trustee renders the employment improper under the circumstances of the case. Whenever under this subdivision an individual may not be approved for appointment or employment, the individual's firm, partnership, corporation, or any other form of business association or relationship, and all members, associates and professional employees thereof also may not be approved for appointment or employment.

(b) **Judicial Determination that Approval of Appointment or Employment Is Improper**. A bankruptcy judge may not approve the appointment of a person as a trustee or examiner pursuant to § 1104 of the Code or approve the employment of a person as an attorney, accountant, appraiser, auctioneer, or other professional person pursuant to §§ 327, 1103, or 1114 of the Code if that person is or has been so connected with such judge or the United States trustee as to render the appointment or employment improper.

Rule 5003. Records Kept by the Clerk

(a) **Bankruptcy Dockets**. The clerk shall keep a docket in each case under the Code and shall enter thereon each judgment, order, and activity in that case as prescribed by the Director of the Administrative Office of the United States Courts. The entry of a judgment or order in a docket shall show the date the entry is made.

(b) **Claims Register**. The clerk shall keep in a claims register a list of claims filed in a case when it appears that there will be a distribution to unsecured creditors.

(c) **Judgments and Orders**. The clerk shall keep, in the form and manner as the Director of the Administrative Office of the United States Courts may prescribe, a correct copy of every final judgment or order affecting title to or lien on real property or for the recovery of money or property, and any other order which the court may direct to be kept. On request of the prevailing party, a correct copy of every judgment or order affecting title to or lien upon real or personal property or for the recovery of money or property shall be kept and indexed with the civil judgments of the district court.

(d) **Index of Cases; Certificate of Search**. The clerk shall keep indices of all cases and adversary proceedings as prescribed by the Director of the Administrative Office of the United States Courts. On request, the clerk shall make a search of any index and papers in the clerk's custody and certify whether a case or proceeding has been filed in or transferred to the court or if a discharge has been entered in its records.

(e) **Register of Mailing Addresses of Federal and State Governmental Units and Certain Taxing Authorities**. The United States or the state or territory in which the court is located may file a statement designating its mailing address. The United States, state, territory, or local governmental unit responsible for collecting taxes within the district in which the case is pending may also file a statement designating an address for service of requests under § 505(b) of the Code, and the designation shall describe where further information concerning additional requirements for filing such requests may be found. The clerk shall keep, in the form and manner as the Director of the Administrative Office of the United States Courts may prescribe, a register that includes the mailing addresses designated under the first sentence of this subdivision, and a separate register of the addresses designated for the service of requests under § 505(b) of the Code. The clerk is not required to include in any single register more than one mailing address for each department, agency, or instrumentality of the United States or the state or territory. If more than one address for a department, agency, or instrumentality is included in the register, the clerk shall also include information that would enable a user of the register to determine the circumstances when each address is applicable, and mailing notice to only one applicable address is sufficient to provide effective notice. The clerk shall update the register annually, effective January 2 of each year. The mailing address in the register is conclusively presumed to be a proper address for the governmental unit, but the failure to use that mailing address does not invalidate any notice that is otherwise effective under applicable law.

(f) **Other Books and Records of the Clerk.** The clerk shall keep any other books and records required by the Director of the Administrative Office of the United States Courts.

Rule 5004. Disqualification

(a) **Disqualification of Judge.** A bankruptcy judge shall be governed by 28 U.S.C. § 455, and disqualified from presiding over the proceeding or contested matter in which the disqualifying circumstances arises or, if appropriate, shall be disqualified from presiding over the case.

(b) **Disqualification of Judge from Allowing Compensation.** A bankruptcy judge shall be disqualified from allowing compensation to a person who is a relative of the bankruptcy judge or with whom the judge is so connected as to render it improper for the judge to authorize such compensation.

Rule 5005. Filing and Transmittal of Papers

(a) **Filing.**

  (1) *Place of Filing.* The lists, schedules, statements, proofs of claim or interest, complaints, motions, applications, objections and other papers required to be filed by these rules, except as provided in 28 U.S.C. § 1409, shall be filed with the clerk in the district where the case under the Code is pending. The judge of that court may permit the papers to be filed with the judge, in which event the filing date shall be noted thereon, and they shall be forthwith transmitted to the clerk. The clerk shall not refuse to accept for filing any petition or other paper presented for the purpose of filing solely because it is not presented in proper form as required by these rules or any local rules or practices.

  (2) *Filing by Electronic Means.* A court may by local rule permit or require documents to be filed, signed, or verified by electronic means that are consistent with technical standards, if any, that the Judicial Conference of the United States establishes. A local rule may require filing by electronic means only if reasonable exceptions are allowed. A document filed by electronic means in compliance with a local rule constitutes a written paper for the purpose of applying these rules, the Federal Rules of Civil Procedure made applicable by these rules, and § 107 of the Code.

(b) **Transmittal to the United States Trustee.**

  (1) The complaints, motions, applications, objections and other papers required to be transmitted to the United States trustee by these rules shall be mailed or delivered to an office of the United States trustee, or to another place designated by the United States trustee, in the district where the case under the Code is pending.

(2) The entity, other than the clerk, transmitting a paper to the United States trustee shall promptly file as proof of such transmittal a verified statement identifying the paper and stating the date on which it was transmitted to the United States trustee.

(3) Nothing in these rules shall require the clerk to transmit any paper to the United States trustee if the United States trustee requests in writing that the paper not be transmitted.

(c) **Error in Filing or Transmittal.** A paper intended to be filed with the clerk but erroneously delivered to the United States trustee, the trustee, the attorney for the trustee, a bankruptcy judge, a district judge, the clerk of the bankruptcy appellate panel, or the clerk of the district court shall, after the date of its receipt has been noted thereon, be transmitted forthwith to the clerk of the bankruptcy court. A paper intended to be transmitted to the United States trustee but erroneously delivered to the clerk, the trustee, the attorney for the trustee, a bankruptcy judge, a district judge, the clerk of the bankruptcy appellate panel, or the clerk of the district court shall, after the date of its receipt has been noted thereon, be transmitted forthwith to the United States trustee. In the interest of justice, the court may order that a paper erroneously delivered shall be deemed filed with the clerk or transmitted to the United States trustee as of the date of its original delivery.

Rule 5006. Certification of Copies of Papers

The clerk shall issue a certified copy of the record of any proceeding in a case under the Code or of any paper filed with the clerk on payment of any prescribed fee.

Rule 5007. Record of Proceedings and Transcripts

(a) **Filing of Record or Transcript.** The reporter or operator of a recording device shall certify the original notes of testimony, tape recording, or other original record of the proceeding and promptly file them with the clerk. The person preparing any transcript shall promptly file a certified copy.

(b) **Transcript Fees.** The fees for copies of transcripts shall be charged at rates prescribed by the Judicial Conference of the United States. No fee may be charged for the certified copy filed with the clerk.

(c) **Admissibility of Record in Evidence.** A certified sound recording or a transcript of a proceeding shall be admissible as prima facie evidence to establish the record.

Rule 5008. Notice Regarding Presumption of Abuse in Chapter 7 Cases of Individual Debtors

If a presumption of abuse has arisen under § 707(b) in a chapter 7 case of an individual with primarily consumer debts, the clerk shall within 10 days after the date of the filing of the petition notify creditors of the presumption of abuse in accordance with Rule 2002. If the debtor has not filed a statement indicating whether a presumption of abuse has arisen, the clerk shall within 10 days after the date of the filing of the petition notify creditors that the debtor has not filed the statement and that further notice will be given if a later filed statement indicates that a presumption of abuse has arisen. If a debtor later files a statement indicating that a presumption of abuse has arisen, the clerk shall notify creditors of the presumption of abuse as promptly as practicable.

Rule 5009. Closing Chapter 7, Chapter 12, Chapter 13, and Chapter 15 Cases; Order Declaring Lien Satisfied

(a) **Closing of Cases under Chapters 7, 12, and 13**. If in a chapter 7, chapter 12, or chapter 13 case the trustee has filed a final report and final account and has certified that the estate has been fully administered, and if within 30 days no objection has been filed by the United States trustee or a party in interest, there shall be a presumption that the estate has been fully administered.

(b) **Notice of Failure to File Rule 1007(b)(7) Statement**. If an individual debtor in a chapter 7 or 13 case is required to file a statement under Rule 1007(b)(7) and fails to do so within 45 days after the first date set for the meeting of creditors under § 341(a) of the Code, the clerk shall promptly notify the debtor that the case will be closed without entry of a discharge unless the required statement is filed within the applicable time limit under Rule 1007(c).

(c) **Cases under Chapter 15**. A foreign representative in a proceeding recognized under § 1517 of the Code shall file a final report when the purpose of the representative's appearance in the court is completed. The report shall describe the nature and results of the representative's activities in the court. The foreign representative shall transmit the report to the United States trustee, and give notice of its filing to the debtor, all persons or bodies authorized to administer foreign proceedings of the debtor, all parties to litigation pending in the United States in which the debtor was a party at the time of the filing of the petition, and such other entities as the court may direct. The foreign representative shall file a certificate with the court that notice has been given. If no objection has been filed by the United States trustee or a party in interest within 30 days after the certificate is filed, there shall be a presumption that the case has been fully administered.

(d) **Order Declaring Lien Satisfied**. In a chapter 12 or chapter 13 case, if a claim that was secured by property of the estate is subject to a lien under applicable nonbankruptcy law, the debtor may request entry of an order declaring that the secured claim has been satisfied and the lien has been released under the terms of a confirmed plan. The request shall be made by motion and shall be served on the holder of the claim and any other entity the court designates in the manner provided by Rule 7004 for service of a summons and complaint.

Rule 5010. Reopening Cases

A case may be reopened on motion of the debtor or other party in interest pursuant to § 350(b) of the Code. In a chapter 7, 12, or 13 case a trustee shall not be appointed by the United States trustee unless the court determines that a trustee is necessary to protect the interests of creditors and the debtor or to insure efficient administration of the case.

Rule 5011. Withdrawal and Abstention from Hearing a Proceeding

(a) **Withdrawal.** A motion for withdrawal of a case or proceeding shall be heard by a district judge.

(b) **Abstention from Hearing a Proceeding.** A motion for abstention pursuant to 28 U.S.C. § 1334(c) shall be governed by Rule 9014 and shall be served on the parties to the proceeding.

(c) **Effect of Filing of Motion for Withdrawal or Abstention.** The filing of a motion for withdrawal of a case or proceeding or for abstention pursuant to 28 U.S.C. § 1334(c)shall not stay the administration of the case or any proceeding therein before the bankruptcy judge except that the bankruptcy judge may stay, on such terms and conditions as are proper, proceedings pending disposition of the motion. A motion for a stay ordinarily shall be presented first to the bankruptcy judge. A motion for a stay or relief from a stay filed in the district court shall state why it has not been presented to or obtained from the bankruptcy judge. Relief granted by the district judge shall be on such terms and conditions as the judge deems proper.

Rule 5012. Agreements Concerning Coordination of Proceedings in Chapter 15 Cases

Approval of an agreement under § 1527(4) of the Code shall be sought by motion. The movant shall attach to the motion a copy of the proposed agreement or protocol and, unless the court directs otherwise, give at least 30 days' notice of any hearing on the motion by transmitting the motion to the United States trustee, and serving it on the debtor, all persons or bodies authorized to administer foreign proceedings of the debtor, all entities against whom provisional relief is being sought under § 1519, all parties to litigation pending in the United States in which the debtor was a party at the time of the filing of the petition, and such other entities as the court may direct.

Part VI. Collection and liquidation of the estate

Rule 6001. Burden of Proof as to Validity of Postpetition Transfer

Any entity asserting the validity of a transfer under § 549 of the Code shall have the burden of proof.

Rule 6002. Accounting by Prior Custodian of Property of the Estate

(a) **Accounting Required.** Any custodian required by the Code to deliver property in the custodian's possession or control to the trustee shall promptly file and transmit to the United States trustee a report and account with respect to the property of the estate and the administration thereof.

(b) **Examination of Administration.** On the filing and transmittal of the report and account required by subdivision (a) of this rule and after an examination has been made into the superseded administration, after notice and a hearing, the court shall determine the propriety of the administration, including the reasonableness of all disbursements.

Rule 6003. Interim and Final Relief Immediately Following the Commencement of the Case-Applications for Employment; Motions for Use, Sale, or Lease of Property; and Motions for Assumption or Assignment of Executory Contracts

Except to the extent that relief is necessary to avoid immediate and irreparable harm, the court shall not, within 21 days after the filing of the petition, issue an order granting the following:

(a) an application under Rule 2014;

(b) a motion to use, sell, lease, or otherwise incur an obligation regarding property of the estate, including a motion to pay all or part of a claim that arose before the filing of the petition, but not a motion under Rule 4001; or

(c) a motion to assume or assign an executory contract or unexpired lease in accordance with § 365.

Rule 6004. Use, Sale, or Lease of Property

(a) **Notice of Proposed Use, Sale, or Lease of Property.** Notice of a proposed use, sale, or lease of property, other than cash collateral, not in the ordinary course of business shall be given pursuant to Rule 2002(a)(2), (c)(1), (i), and (k) and, if applicable, in accordance with § 363(b)(2) of the Code.

(b) **Objection to Proposal.** Except as provided in subdivisions (c) and (d) of this rule, an objection to a proposed use, sale, or lease of property shall be filed and served not less than seven days before the date set for the proposed action or within the time fixed by the court. An objection to the proposed use, sale, or lease of property is governed by Rule 9014.

(c) **Sale Free and Clear of Liens and Other Interests**. A motion for authority to sell property free and clear of liens or other interests shall be made in accordance with Rule 9014 and shall be served on the parties who have liens or other interests in the property to be sold. The notice required by subdivision (a) of this rule shall include the date of the hearing on the motion and the time within which objections may be filed and served on the debtor in possession or trustee.

(d) **Sale of Property Under $2,500**. Notwithstanding subdivision (a) of this rule, when all of the nonexempt property of the estate has an aggregate gross value less than $2,500, it shall be sufficient to give a general notice of intent to sell such property other than in the ordinary course of business to all creditors, indenture trustees, committees appointed or elected pursuant to the Code, the United States trustee and other persons as the court may direct. An objection to any such sale may be filed and served by a party in interest within 14 days of the mailing of the notice, or within the time fixed by the court. An objection is governed by Rule 9014.

(e) **Hearing**. If a timely objection is made pursuant to subdivision (b) or (d) of this rule, the date of the hearing thereon may be set in the notice given pursuant to subdivision (a) of this rule.

(f) **Conduct of Sale Not in the Ordinary Course of Business**.

(1) *Public or Private Sale*. All sales not in the ordinary course of business may be by private sale or by public auction. Unless it is impracticable, an itemized statement of the property sold, the name of each purchaser, and the price received for each item or lot or for the property as a whole if sold in bulk shall be filed on completion of a sale. If the property is sold by an auctioneer, the auctioneer shall file the statement, transmit a copy thereof to the United States trustee, and furnish a copy to the trustee, debtor in possession, or chapter 13 debtor. If the property is not sold by an auctioneer, the trustee, debtor in possession, or chapter 13 debtor shall file the statement and transmit a copy thereof to the United States trustee.

(2) *Execution of Instruments*. After a sale in accordance with this rule the debtor, the trustee, or debtor in possession, as the case may be, shall execute any instrument necessary or ordered by the court to effectuate the transfer to the purchaser.

(g) **Sale of Personally Identifiable Information**.

(1) *Motion*. A motion for authority to sell or lease personally identifiable information under § 363(b)(1)(B) shall include a request for an order directing the United States trustee to appoint a consumer privacy ombudsman under § 332. Rule 9014 governs the motion which shall be served on: any committee elected under § 705 or appointed under § 1102 of the Code, or if the case is a chapter 11 reorganization case and no committee of unsecured creditors has been appointed under § 1102, on the creditors included on the list of creditors filed under

Rule 1007(d); and on such other entities as the court may direct. The motion shall be transmitted to the United States trustee.

(2) *Appointment.* If a consumer privacy ombudsman is appointed under § 332, no later than seven days before the hearing on the motion under § 363(b)(1)(B), the United States trustee shall file a notice of the appointment, including the name and address of the person appointed. The United States trustee's notice shall be accompanied by a verified statement of the person appointed setting forth the person's connections with the debtor, creditors, any other party in interest, their respective attorneys and accountants, the United States trustee, or any person employed in the office of the United States trustee.

(h) **Stay of Order Authorizing Use, Sale, or Lease of Property.** An order authorizing the use, sale, or lease of property other than cash collateral is stayed until the expiration of 14 days after entry of the order, unless the court orders otherwise.

Rule 6005. Appraisers and Auctioneers

The order of the court approving the employment of an appraiser or auctioneer shall fix the amount or rate of compensation. No officer or employee of the Judicial Branch of the United States or the United States Department of Justice shall be eligible to act as appraiser or auctioneer. No residence or licensing requirement shall disqualify an appraiser or auctioneer from employment.

Rule 6006. Assumption, Rejection or Assignment of an Executory Contract or Unexpired Lease

(a) **Proceeding to Assume, Reject, or Assign.** A proceeding to assume, reject, or assign an executory contract or unexpired lease, other than as part of a plan, is governed by Rule 9014.

(b) **Proceeding to Require Trustee to Act.** A proceeding by a party to an executory contract or unexpired lease in a chapter 9 municipality case, chapter 11 reorganization case, Chapter 12 family farmer's debt adjustment case, or chapter 13 individual's debt adjustment case, to require the trustee, debtor in possession, or debtor to determine whether to assume or reject the contract or lease is governed by Rule 9014.

(c) **Notice.** Notice of a motion made pursuant to subdivision (a) or (b) of this rule shall be given to the other party to the contract or lease, to other parties in interest as the court may direct, and, except in a chapter 9 municipality case, to the United States trustee.

(d) **Stay of Order Authorizing Assignment.** An order authorizing the trustee to assign an executory contract or unexpired lease under § 365(f) is stayed until the expiration of 14 days after the entry of the order, unless the court orders otherwise.

(e) **Limitations.** The trustee shall not seek authority to assume or assign multiple executory contracts or unexpired leases in one motion unless: (1) all executory contracts or unexpired leases to be assumed or assigned are between the same parties or are to be assigned to the same assignee; (2) the trustee seeks to assume, but not assign to more than one assignee, unexpired leases of real property; or (3) the court otherwise authorizes the motion to be filed. Subject to subdivision (f), the trustee may join requests for authority to reject multiple executory contracts or unexpired leases in one motion.

(f) **Omnibus Motions.** A motion to reject or, if permitted under subdivision (e), a motion to assume or assign multiple executory contracts or unexpired leases that are not between the same parties shall:

    (1) state in a conspicuous place that parties receiving the omnibus motion should locate their names and their contracts or leases listed in the motion;

    (2) list parties alphabetically and identify the corresponding contract or lease;

    (3) specify the terms, including the curing of defaults, for each requested assumption or assignment;

    (4) specify the terms, including the identity of each assignee and the adequate assurance of future performance by each assignee, for each requested assignment;

    (5) be numbered consecutively with other omnibus motions to assume, assign, or reject executory contracts or unexpired leases; and

    (6) be limited to no more than 100 executory contracts or unexpired leases.

(g) **Finality of Determination.** The finality of any order respecting an executory contract or unexpired lease included in an omnibus motion shall be determined as though such contract or lease had been the subject of a separate motion.

Rule 6007. Abandonment or Disposition of Property

(a) **Notice of Proposed Abandonment or Disposition; Objections; Hearing.** Unless otherwise directed by the court, the trustee or debtor in possession shall give notice of a proposed abandonment or disposition of property to the United States trustee, all creditors, indenture trustees, and committees elected pursuant to § 705 or appointed pursuant to § 1102 of the Code. A party in interest may file and serve an objection within 14 days of the mailing of the notice, or within the time fixed by the court. If a timely objection is made, the court shall set a hearing on notice to the United States trustee and to other entities as the court may direct.

(b) **Motion by Party in Interest.** A party in interest may file and serve a motion requiring the trustee or debtor in possession to abandon property of the estate.

(c) [Abrogated]

Rule 6008. Redemption of Property from Lien or Sale

On motion by the debtor, trustee, or debtor in possession and after hearing on notice as the court may direct, the court may authorize the redemption of property from a lien or from a sale to enforce a lien in accordance with applicable law.

Rule 6009. Prosecution and Defense of Proceedings by Trustee or Debtor in Possession

With or without court approval, the trustee or debtor in possession may prosecute or may enter an appearance and defend any pending action or proceeding by or against the debtor, or commence and prosecute any action or proceeding in behalf of the estate before any tribunal.

Rule 6010. Proceeding to Avoid Indemnifying Lien or Transfer to Surety

If a lien voidable under § 547 of the Code has been dissolved by the furnishing of a bond or other obligation and the surety thereon has been indemnified by the transfer of, or the creation of a lien upon, nonexempt property of the debtor, the surety shall be joined as a defendant in any proceeding to avoid the indemnifying transfer or lien. Such proceeding is governed by the rules in Part VII.

Rule 6011. Disposal of Patient Records in Health Care Business Case

(a) **Notice by Publication Under § 351(1)(A).** A notice regarding the claiming or disposing of patient records under § 351(1)(A) shall not identify any patient by name or other identifying information, but shall:

    (1) identify with particularity the health care facility whose patient records the trustee proposes to destroy;

    (2) state the name, address, telephone number, email address, and website, if any, of a person from whom information about the patient records may be obtained;

    (3) state how to claim the patient records; and

    (4) state the date by which patient records must be claimed, and that if they are not so claimed the records will be destroyed.

(b) **Notice by Mail Under § 351(1)(B).** Subject to applicable nonbankruptcy law relating to patient privacy, a notice regarding the claiming or disposing of patient records under § 351(1)(B) shall, in addition to including the information in subdivision (a), direct that a patient's family member or other representative who receives the notice inform the patient of the notice. Any notice under this subdivision shall be mailed to the patient and any family member or other contact person whose name and address have been given to the trustee or the debtor for the purpose of providing information regarding the patient's health care, to the Attorney General of the State where the health care facility is located, and to any insurance company known to have provided health care insurance to the patient.

(c) **Proof of Compliance with Notice Requirement.** Unless the court orders the trustee to file proof of compliance with § 351(1)(B) under seal, the trustee shall not file, but shall maintain, the proof of compliance for a reasonable time.

(d) **Report of Destruction of Records.** The trustee shall file, no later than 30 days after the destruction of patient records under § 351(3), a report certifying that the unclaimed records have been destroyed and explaining the method used to effect the destruction. The report shall not identify any patient by name or other identifying information.

Part VII. Adversary proceedings

Rule 7001. Scope of Rules of Part VII

An adversary proceeding is governed by the rules of this Part VII. The following are adversary proceedings:
(1) a proceeding to recover money or property, other than a proceeding to compel the debtor to deliver property to the trustee, or a proceeding under § 554(b) or § 725 of the Code, Rule 2017, or Rule 6002;
(2) a proceeding to determine the validity, priority, or extent of a lien or other interest in property, but not a proceeding under Rule 3012 or Rule 4003(d);
(3) a proceeding to obtain approval under § 363(h) for the sale of both the interest of the estate and of a co-owner in property;
(4) a proceeding to object to or revoke a discharge, other than an objection to discharge under §§ 727(a)(8), (a)(9), or 1328(f);
(5) a proceeding to revoke an order of confirmation of a chapter 11, chapter 12 or chapter 13 plan;
(6) a proceeding to determine the dischargeability of a debt;
(7) a proceeding to obtain an injunction or other equitable relief, except when a chapter 9, chapter 11, chapter 12, or chapter 13 plan provides for the relief;
(8) a proceeding to subordinate any allowed claim or interest, except when a chapter 9, chapter 11, chapter 12, or chapter 13 plan provides for subordination;
(9) a proceeding to obtain a declaratory judgment relating to any of the foregoing; or
(10) a proceeding to determine a claim or cause of action removed under 28 U.S.C. § 1452.

Rule 7002. References to Federal Rules of Civil Procedure

Whenever a Federal Rule of Civil Procedure applicable to adversary proceedings makes reference to another Federal Rule of Civil Procedure, the reference shall be read as a reference to the Federal Rule of Civil Procedure as modified in this Part VII.

Rule 7003. Commencement of Adversary Proceeding

Rule 3 F. R. Civ. P. applies in adversary proceedings.

Rule 7004. Process; Service of Summons, Complaint

(a) **Summons; Service; Proof of Service**.
    (1) Except as provided in Rule 7004(a)(2), Rule 4(a), (b), (c)(1), (d)(1), (e)-(j), (l), and (m) F. R. Civ. P. applies in adversary proceedings. Personal service under Rule 4(e)-(j) F. R. Civ. P. may be made by any

person at least 18 years of age who is not a party, and the summons may be delivered by the clerk to any such person.

(2) The clerk may sign, seal, and issue a summons electronically by putting an "s/" before the clerk's name and including the court's seal on the summons.

(b) **Service by First Class Mail**. Except as provided in subdivision (h), in addition to the methods of service authorized by Rule 4(e)-(j) F. R. Civ. P., service may be made within the United States by first class mail postage prepaid as follows:

(1) Upon an individual other than an infant or incompetent, by mailing a copy of the summons and complaint to the individual's dwelling house or usual place of abode or to the place where the individual regularly conducts a business or profession.

(2) Upon an infant or an incompetent person, by mailing a copy of the summons and complaint to the person upon whom process is prescribed to be served by the law of the state in which service is made when an action is brought against such a defendant in the courts of general jurisdiction of that state. The summons and complaint in that case shall be addressed to the person required to be served at that person's dwelling house or usual place of abode or at the place where the person regularly conducts a business or profession.

(3) Upon a domestic or foreign corporation or upon a partnership or other unincorporated association, by mailing a copy of the summons and complaint to the attention of an officer, a managing or general agent, or to any other agent authorized by appointment or by law to receive service of process and, if the agent is one authorized by statute to receive service and the statute so requires, by also mailing a copy to the defendant.

(4) Upon the United States, by mailing a copy of the summons and complaint addressed to the civil process clerk at the office of the United States attorney for the district in which the action is brought and by mailing a copy of the summons and complaint to the Attorney General of the United States at Washington, District of Columbia, and in any action attacking the validity of an order of an officer or an agency of the United States not made a party, by also mailing a copy of the summons and complaint to that officer or agency. The court shall allow a reasonable time for service pursuant to this subdivision for the purpose of curing the failure to mail a copy of the summons and complaint to multiple officers, agencies, or corporations of the United States if the plaintiff has mailed a copy of the summons and complaint either to the civil process clerk at the office of the United States attorney or to the Attorney General of the United States.

(5) Upon any officer or agency of the United States, by mailing a copy of the summons and complaint to the United States as prescribed in paragraph (4) of this subdivision and also to the officer or agency. If the agency is a corporation, the mailing shall be as prescribed in paragraph (3) of this subdivision of this rule. The court shall allow a

reasonable time for service pursuant to this subdivision for the purpose of curing the failure to mail a copy of the summons and complaint to multiple officers, agencies, or corporations of the United States if the plaintiff has mailed a copy of the summons and complaint either to the civil process clerk at the office of the United States attorney or to the Attorney General of the United States. If the United States trustee is the trustee in the case and service is made upon the United States trustee solely as trustee, service may be made as prescribed in paragraph (10) of this subdivision of this rule.

(6) Upon a state or municipal corporation or other governmental organization thereof subject to suit, by mailing a copy of the summons and complaint to the person or office upon whom process is prescribed to be served by the law of the state in which service is made when an action is brought against such a defendant in the courts of general jurisdiction of that state, or in the absence of the designation of any such person or office by state law, then to the chief executive officer thereof.

(7) Upon a defendant of any class referred to in paragraph (1) or (3) of this subdivision of this rule, it is also sufficient if a copy of the summons and complaint is mailed to the entity upon whom service is prescribed to be served by any statute of the United States or by the law of the state in which service is made when an action is brought against such a defendant in the court of general jurisdiction of that state.

(8) Upon any defendant, it is also sufficient if a copy of the summons and complaint is mailed to an agent of such defendant authorized by appointment or by law to receive service of process, at the agent's dwelling house or usual place of abode or at the place where the agent regularly carries on a business or profession and, if the authorization so requires, by mailing also a copy of the summons and complaint to the defendant as provided in this subdivision.

(9) Upon the debtor, after a petition has been filed by or served upon the debtor and until the case is dismissed or closed, by mailing a copy of the summons and complaint to the debtor at the address shown in the petition or to such other address as the debtor may designate in a filed writing.

(10) Upon the United States trustee, when the United States trustee is the trustee in the case and service is made upon the United States trustee solely as trustee, by mailing a copy of the summons and complaint to an office of the United States trustee or another place designated by the United States trustee in the district where the case under the Code is pending.

(c) **Service by Publication**. If a party to an adversary proceeding to determine or protect rights in property in the custody of the court cannot be served as provided in Rule 4(e)-(j) F. R. Civ. P. or subdivision (b) of this rule, the court may order the summons and complaint to be served by mailing copies thereof by first class mail postage prepaid, to the party's last known address and by at least one publication in such manner and form as the court may direct.

(d) **Nationwide Service of Process.** The summons and complaint and all other process except a subpoena may be served anywhere in the United States.

(e) **Summons: Time Limit for Service Within the United States.** Service made under Rule 4(e), (g), (h)(1), (i), or (j)(2) F. R. Civ. P. shall be by delivery of the summons and complaint within 7 days after the summons is issued. If service is by any authorized form of mail, the summons and complaint shall be deposited in the mail within 7 days after the summons is issued. If a summons is not timely delivered or mailed, another summons will be issued for service. This subdivision does not apply to service in a foreign country.

(f) **Personal Jurisdiction.** If the exercise of jurisdiction is consistent with the Constitution and laws of the United States, serving a summons or filing a waiver of service in accordance with this rule or the subdivisions of Rule 4 F. R. Civ. P. made applicable by these rules is effective to establish personal jurisdiction over the person of any defendant with respect to a case under the Code or a civil proceeding arising under the Code, or arising in or related to a case under the Code.

(g) **Service on Debtor's Attorney.** If the debtor is represented by an attorney, whenever service is made upon the debtor under this Rule, service shall also be made upon the debtor's attorney by any means authorized under Rule 5(b) F. R. Civ. P.

(h) **Service of Process on an Insured Depository Institution.** Service on an insured depository institution (as defined in section 3 of the Federal Deposit Insurance Act) in a contested matter or adversary proceeding shall be made by certified mail addressed to an officer of the institution unless

   (1) the institution has appeared by its attorney, in which case the attorney shall be served by first class mail;

   (2) the court orders otherwise after service upon the institution by certified mail of notice of an application to permit service on the institution by first class mail sent to an officer of the institution designated by the institution; or

   (3) the institution has waived in writing its entitlement to service by certified mail by designating an officer to receive service.

Rule 7005. Service and Filing of Pleadings and Other Papers

Rule 5 F. R. Civ. P. applies in adversary proceedings.

Rule 7007. Pleadings Allowed

Rule 7 F. R. Civ. P. applies in adversary proceedings.

Rule 7007.1. Corporate Ownership Statement

(a) Required Disclosure. Any corporation that is a party to an adversary proceeding, other than the debtor or a governmental unit, shall file two copies of a statement that identifies any corporation, other than a governmental unit, that directly or indirectly owns 10% or more of any class of the corporation's equity interests, or states that there are no entities to report under this subdivision.

(b) Time for Filing. A party shall file the statement required under Rule 7007.1(a) with its first appearance, pleading, motion, response, or other request addressed to the court. A party shall file a supplemental statement promptly upon any change in circumstances that this rule requires the party to identify or disclose.

Rule 7008. General Rules of Pleading

Rule 8 F. R. Civ. P. applies in adversary proceedings. The allegation of jurisdiction required by Rule 8(a) shall also contain a reference to the name, number, and chapter of the case under the Code to which the adversary proceeding relates and to the district and division where the case under the Code is pending. In an adversary proceeding before a bankruptcy court, the complaint, counterclaim, cross-claim, or third-party complaint shall contain a statement that the pleader does or does not consent to entry of final orders or judgment by the bankruptcy court.

Rule 7009. Pleading Special Matters

Rule 9 F. R. Civ. P. applies in adversary proceedings.

Rule 7010. Form of Pleadings

Rule 10 F. R. Civ. P. applies in adversary proceedings, except that the caption of each pleading in such a proceeding shall conform substantially to the appropriate Official Form.

Rule 7012. Defenses and Objections—When and How Presented—by Pleading or Motion-Motion for Judgment on the Pleadings

(a) **When Presented**. If a complaint is duly served, the defendant shall serve an answer within 30 days after the issuance of the summons, except when a different time is prescribed by the court. The court shall prescribe the time for service of the answer when service of a complaint is made by publication or upon a party in a foreign country. A party served with a pleading stating a cross-claim shall serve an answer thereto within 21 days after service. The plaintiff shall serve a reply to a counterclaim in the answer within 21 days after service of the answer or, if a reply is ordered by the court, within 21 days after service of the order, unless the order otherwise directs. The United States or an officer or agency thereof shall serve an answer to a complaint within 35 days after the issuance of the summons, and shall serve an answer to a cross-claim, or a reply to a counterclaim, within 35 days after service upon the United States attorney of the pleading in which the claim is asserted. The service of a motion permitted under this rule alters these periods of time as follows, unless a different time is fixed by order of the court: (1) if the court denies the motion or postpones its disposition until the trial on the merits, the responsive pleading shall be served within 14 days after notice of the court's action; (2) if the court grants a motion for a more definite statement, the responsive pleading shall be served within 14 days after the service of a more definite statement.

(b) **Applicability of Rule 12(b)-(i) F. R. Civ. P**. Rule 12(b)-(i) F. R. Civ. P. applies in adversary proceedings. A responsive pleading shall include a statement that the party does or does not consent to entry of final orders or judgment by the bankruptcy court.

Rule 7013. Counterclaim and Cross-Claim

Rule 13 F. R. Civ. P. applies in adversary proceedings, except that a party sued by a trustee or debtor in possession need not state as a counterclaim any claim that the party has against the debtor, the debtor's property, or the estate, unless the claim arose after the entry of an order for relief. A trustee or debtor in possession who fails to plead a counterclaim through oversight, inadvertence, or excusable neglect, or when justice so requires, may by leave of court amend the pleading, or commence a new adversary proceeding or separate action.

Rule 7014. Third-Party Practice

Rule 14 F. R. Civ. P. applies in adversary proceedings.

Rule 7015. Amended and Supplemental Pleadings

Rule 15 F. R. Civ. P. applies in adversary proceedings.

Rule 7016. Pre-trial Procedures

(a) **Pretrial Conferences; Scheduling; Management.** Rule 16 F. R. Civ. P. applies in adversary proceedings.

(b) **Determining Procedure.** The bankruptcy court shall decide, on its own motion or a party's timely motion, whether
    (1) to hear and determine the proceeding;
    (2) to hear the proceeding and issue proposed findings of fact and conclusions of law; or
    (3) to take some other action.

Rule 7017. Parties Plaintiff and Defendant; Capacity

Rule 17 F. R. Civ. P. applies in adversary proceedings, except as provided in Rule 2010(b).

Rule 7018. Joinder of Claims and Remedies

Rule 18 F. R. Civ. P. applies in adversary proceedings.

Rule 7019. Joinder of Persons Needed for Just Determination

Rule 19 F. R. Civ. P. applies in adversary proceedings, except that (1) if an entity joined as a party raises the defense that the court lacks jurisdiction over the subject matter and the defense is sustained, the court shall dismiss such entity from the adversary proceeding and (2) if an entity joined as a party properly and timely raises the defense of improper venue, the court shall determine, as provided in 28 U.S.C. § 1412, whether that part of the proceeding involving the joined party shall be transferred to another district, or whether the entire adversary proceeding shall be transferred to another district.

Rule 7020. Permissive Joinder of Parties

Rule 20 F. R. Civ. P. applies in adversary proceedings.

Rule 7021. Misjoinder and Non-Joinder of Parties

Rule 21 F. R. Civ. P. applies in adversary proceedings.

Rule 7022. Interpleader

Rule 22 (a) F. R. Civ. P. applies in adversary proceedings. This rule supplements—and does not limit—the joinder of parties allowed by Rule 7020.

Rule 7023. Class Proceedings

Rule 23 F. R. Civ. P. applies in adversary proceedings.

Rule 7023.1. Derivative Actions

Rule 23.1 F. R. Civ. P. applies in adversary proceedings.

Rule 7023.2. Adversary Proceedings Relating to Unincorporated Associations

Rule 23.2 F. R. Civ. P. applies in adversary proceedings.

Rule 7024. Intervention

Rule 24 F. R. Civ. P. applies in adversary proceedings.

Rule 7025. Substitution of Parties

Subject to the provisions of Rule 2012, Rule 25 F. R. Civ. P. applies in adversary proceedings.

Rule 7026. General Provisions Governing Discovery

F. R. Civ. P. applies in adversary proceedings.

Rule 7027. Depositions Before Adversary Proceedings or Pending Appeal

Rule 27 F. R. Civ. P. applies in adversary proceedings.

Rule 7028. Persons Before Whom Depositions May Be Taken

Rule 28 F. R. Civ. P. applies in adversary proceedings.

Rule 7029. Stipulations Regarding Discovery Procedure

Rule 29 F. R. Civ. P. applies in adversary proceedings.

Rule 7030. Depositions Upon Oral Examination

Rule 30 F. R. Civ. P. applies in adversary proceedings.

Rule 7031. Deposition Upon Written Questions

Rule 31 F. R. Civ. P. applies in adversary proceedings.

Rule 7032. Use of Depositions in Adversary Proceedings

Rule 32 F. R. Civ. P. applies in adversary proceedings.

Rule 7033. Interrogatories to Parties

Rule 33 F. R. Civ. P. applies in adversary proceedings.

Rule 7034. Production of Documents and Things and Entry Upon Land for Inspection and Other Purposes

Rule 34 F. R. Civ. P. applies in adversary proceedings.

Rule 7035. Physical and Mental Examination of Persons

Rule 35 F. R. Civ. P. applies in adversary proceedings.

Rule 7036. Requests for Admission

F. R. Civ. P. applies in adversary proceedings.

Rule 7037. Failure to Make Discovery: Sanctions

Rule 37 F. R. Civ. P. applies in adversary proceedings.

Rule 7040. Assignment of Cases for Trial

Rule 40 F. R. Civ. P. applies in adversary proceedings.

Rule 7041. Dismissal of Adversary Proceedings

Rule 41 F. R. Civ. P. applies in adversary proceedings, except that a complaint objecting to the debtor's discharge shall not be dismissed at the plaintiff's instance without notice to the trustee, the United States trustee, and such other persons as the court may direct, and only on order of the court containing terms and conditions which the court deems proper.

Rule 7042. Consolidation of Adversary Proceedings; Separate Trials

Rule 42 F. R. Civ. P. applies in adversary proceedings.

Rule 7052. Findings by the Court

Rule 52 F. R. Civ. P. applies in adversary proceedings, except that any motion under subdivision (b) of that rule for amended or additional findings shall be filed no later than 14 days after entry of judgment. In these proceedings, the reference in Rule 52 F. R. Civ. P. to the entry of judgment under Rule 58 F. R. Civ. P. shall be read as a reference to the entry of a judgment or order under Rule 5003(a).

Rule 7054. Judgments; Costs

(a) **Judgments**. Rule 54(a)-(c) F. R. Civ. P. applies in adversary proceedings.
(b) **Costs**.
    (1) *Costs Other Than Attorney's Fees*. The court may allow costs to the prevailing party except when a statute of the United States or these rules otherwise provides. Costs against the United States, its officers and agencies shall be imposed only to the extent permitted by law. Costs may be taxed by the clerk on 14 days' notice; on motion served within seven days thereafter, the action of the clerk may be reviewed by the court.
    (2) *Attorney's Fees*.
        (A) Rule 54(d)(2)(A)-(C) and (E) F. R. Civ. P. applies in adversary proceedings except for the reference in Rule 54(d)(2)(C) to Rule 78.
        (B) By local rule, the court may establish special procedures to resolve fee-related issues without extensive evidentiary hearings.

Rule 7055. Default

Rule 55 F. R. Civ. P. applies in adversary proceedings.

Rule 7056. Summary Judgment

Rule 56 F. R. Civ. P. applies in adversary proceedings, except that any motion for summary judgment must be made at least 30 days before the initial date set for an evidentiary hearing on any issue for which summary judgment is sought, unless a different time is set by local rule or the court orders otherwise.

Rule 7058. Entering Judgment in Adversary Proceeding

Rule 58 F. R. Civ. P. applies in adversary proceedings. In these proceedings, the reference in Rule 58 F. R. Civ. P. to the civil docket shall be read as a reference to the docket maintained by the clerk under Rule 5003(a).

Rule 7062. Stay of Proceedings to Enforce a Judgment

Rule 62 F. R. Civ. P. applies in adversary proceedings.

Rule 7064. Seizure of Person or Property

Rule 64 F. R. Civ. P. applies in adversary proceedings.

Rule 7065. Injunctions

Rule 65 F. R. Civ. P. applies in adversary proceedings, except that a temporary restraining order or preliminary injunction may be issued on application of a debtor, trustee, or debtor in possession without compliance with Rule 65(c).

Rule 7067. Deposit in Court

Rule 67 F. R. Civ. P. applies in adversary proceedings.

Rule 7068. Offer of Judgment

Rule 68 F. R. Civ. P. applies in adversary proceedings.

Rule 7069. Execution

Rule 69 F. R. Civ. P. applies in adversary proceedings.

Rule 7070. Judgment for Specific Acts; Vesting Title

Rule 70 F. R. Civ. P. applies in adversary proceedings and the court may enter a judgment divesting the title of any party and vesting title in others whenever the real or personal property involved is within the jurisdiction of the court.

Rule 7071. Process in Behalf of and Against Persons Not Parties

Rule 71 F. R. Civ. P. applies in adversary proceedings.

Rule 7087. Transfer of Adversary Proceeding

On motion and after a hearing, the court may transfer an adversary proceeding or any part thereof to another district pursuant to 28 U.S.C. § 1412, except as provided in Rule 7019(2).

Part VIII. Appeals to district court or bankruptcy appellate panel

Rule 8001. Scope of Part VIII Rules; Definition of "BAP"; Method of Transmission

(a) **General Scope.** These Part VIII rules govern the procedure in a United States district court and a bankruptcy appellate panel on appeal from a judgment, order, or decree of a bankruptcy court. They also govern certain procedures on appeal to a United States court of appeals under 28 U.S.C. § 158(d).

(b) **Definition of "BAP."** "BAP" means a bankruptcy appellate panel established by a circuit's judicial council and authorized to hear appeals from a bankruptcy court under 28 U.S.C. § 158.

(c) **Method of Transmitting Documents.** A document must be sent electronically under these Part VIII rules, unless it is being sent by or to an individual who is not represented by counsel or the court's governing rules permit or require mailing or other means of delivery.

Rule 8002. Time for Filing Notice of Appeal

(a) **In General.**

(1) *Fourteen-Day Period.* Except as provided in subdivisions (b) and (c), a notice of appeal must be filed with the bankruptcy clerk within 14 days after entry of the judgment, order, or decree being appealed.

(2) *Filing Before the Entry of Judgment.* A notice of appeal filed after the bankruptcy court announces a decision or order—but before entry of the judgment, order, or decree—is treated as filed on the date of and after the entry.

(3) *Multiple Appeals.* If one party files a timely notice of appeal, any other party may file a notice of appeal within 14 days after the date when the first notice was filed, or within the time otherwise allowed by this rule, whichever period ends later.

(4) *Mistaken Filing in Another Court.* If a notice of appeal is mistakenly filed in a district court, BAP, or court of appeals, the clerk of that court must state on the notice the date on which it was received and transmit it to the bankruptcy clerk. The notice of appeal is then considered filed in the bankruptcy court on the date so stated.

(b) **Effect of a Motion on the Time to Appeal.**

(1) *In General.* If a party timely files in the bankruptcy court any of the following motions, the time to file an appeal runs for all parties from the entry of the order disposing of the last such remaining motion:

    (A) to amend or make additional findings under Rule 7052, whether or not granting the motion would alter the judgment;

    (B) to alter or amend the judgment under Rule 9023;

    (C) for a new trial under Rule 9023; or (D) for relief under Rule 9024 if the motion is filed within 14 days after the judgment is entered.

(2) *Filing an Appeal Before the Motion is Decided.* If a party files a notice of appeal after the court announces or enters a judgment, order, or decree—but before it disposes of any motion listed in subdivision (b)(1)—the notice becomes effective when the order disposing of the last such remaining motion is entered.

(3) *Appealing the Ruling on the Motion.* If a party intends to challenge an order disposing of any motion listed in subdivision (b)(1)—or the alteration or amendment of a judgment, order, or decree upon the motion—the party must file a notice of appeal or an amended notice of appeal. The notice or amended notice must comply with Rule 8003 or 8004 and be filed within the time prescribed by this rule, measured from the entry of the order disposing of the last such remaining motion. (4) No Additional Fee. No additional fee is required to file an amended notice of appeal.

(c) **Appeal by an Inmate Confined in an Institution.**

    (1) *In General.* If an inmate confined in an institution files a notice of appeal from a judgment, order, or decree of a bankruptcy court, the notice is timely if it is deposited in the institution's internal mail system on or before the last day for filing. If the institution has a system designed for legal mail, the inmate must use that system to receive the benefit of this rule. Timely filing may be shown by a declaration in compliance with 28 U.S.C. § 1746 or by a notarized statement, either of which must set forth the date of deposit and state that first-class postage has been prepaid.

    (2) *Multiple Appeals.* If an inmate files under this subdivision the first notice of appeal, the 14-day period provided in subdivision (a)(3) for another party to file a notice of appeal runs from the date when the bankruptcy clerk dockets the first notice.

(d) **Extending the Time to Appeal.**

    (1) *When the Time May be Extended.* Except as provided in subdivision (d)(2), the bankruptcy court may extend the time to file a notice of appeal upon a party's motion that is filed:

        (A) within the time prescribed by this rule; or

        (B) within 21 days after that time, if the party shows excusable neglect.

    (2) *When the Time May Not be Extended.* The bankruptcy court may not extend the time to file a notice of appeal if the judgment, order, or decree appealed from:

      (A) grants relief from an automatic stay under § 362, 922, 1201, or 1301 of the Code;

      (B) authorizes the sale or lease of property or the use of cash collateral under § 363 of the Code;

      (C) authorizes the obtaining of credit under § 364 of the Code;

      (D) authorizes the assumption or assignment of an executory contract or unexpired lease under § 365 of the Code;

      (E) approves a disclosure statement under § 1125 of the Code; or

      (F) confirms a plan under § 943, 1129, 1225, or 1325 of the Code.

   (3) *Time Limits on an Extension.* No extension of time may exceed 21 days after the time prescribed by this rule, or 14 days after the order granting the motion to extend time is entered, whichever is later.

Rule 8003. Appeal as of Right-How Taken; Docketing the Appeal

(a) **Filing the Notice of Appeal**.

   (1) *In General.* An appeal from a judgment, order, or decree of a bankruptcy court to a district court or BAP under 28 U.S.C. § 158(a)(1) or (a)(2) may be taken only by filing a notice of appeal with the bankruptcy clerk within the time allowed by Rule 8002.

   (2) *Effect of Not Taking Other Steps.* An appellant's failure to take any step other than the timely filing of a notice of appeal does not affect the validity of the appeal, but is ground only for the district court or BAP to act as it considers appropriate, including dismissing the appeal.

   (3) *Contents.* The notice of appeal must:

      (A) conform substantially to the appropriate Official Form;

      (B) be accompanied by the judgment, order, or decree, or the part of it, being appealed; and

      (C) be accompanied by the prescribed fee.

   (4) *Additional Copies.* If requested to do so, the appellant must furnish the bankruptcy clerk with enough copies of the notice to enable the clerk to comply with subdivision (c).

(b) **Joint or Consolidated Appeals**.

   (1) *Joint Notice of Appeal.* When two or more parties are entitled to appeal from a judgment, order, or decree of a bankruptcy court and their interests make joinder practicable, they may file a joint notice of appeal. They may then proceed on appeal as a single appellant.

   (2) *Consolidating Appeals.* When parties have separately filed timely notices of appeal, the district court or BAP may join or consolidate the appeals.

(c) **Serving the Notice of Appeal**.

   (1) *Serving Parties and Transmitting to the United States Trustee.* The bankruptcy clerk must serve the notice of appeal on counsel of record for each party to the appeal, excluding the appellant, and transmit it to the United States trustee. If a party is proceeding pro se, the clerk must send the notice of appeal to the party's last known address. The

clerk must note, on each copy, the date when the notice of appeal was filed.

(2) *Effect of Failing to Serve or Transmit Notice*. The bankruptcy clerk's failure to serve notice on a party or transmit notice to the United States trustee does not affect the validity of the appeal.

(3) *Noting Service on the Docket*. The clerk must note on the docket the names of the parties served and the date and method of the service.

(d) **Transmitting the Notice of Appeal to the District Court or BAP; Docketing the Appeal**.

(1) *Transmitting the Notice*. The bankruptcy clerk must promptly transmit the notice of appeal to the BAP clerk if a BAP has been established for appeals from that district and the appellant has not elected to have the district court hear the appeal. Otherwise, the bankruptcy clerk must promptly transmit the notice to the district clerk.

(2) *Docketing in the District Court or BAP*. Upon receiving the notice of appeal, the district or BAP clerk must docket the appeal under the title of the bankruptcy case and the title of any adversary proceeding, and must identify the appellant, adding the appellant's name if necessary.

Rule 8004. Appeal by Leave-How Taken; Docketing the Appeal

(a) **Notice of Appeal and Motion for Leave to Appeal**. To appeal from an interlocutory order or decree of a bankruptcy court under 28 U.S.C. § 158(a)(3), a party must file with the bankruptcy clerk a notice of appeal as prescribed by Rule 8003(a). The notice must:

(1) be filed within the time allowed by Rule 8002;

(2) be accompanied by a motion for leave to appeal prepared in accordance with subdivision (b); and

(3) unless served electronically using the court's transmission equipment, include proof of service in accordance with Rule 8011(d).

(b) **Contents of the Motion; Response**.

(1) *Contents*. A motion for leave to appeal under 28 U.S.C. § 158(a)(3) must include the following:

(A) the facts necessary to understand the question presented;

(B) the question itself;

(C) the relief sought;

(D) the reasons why leave to appeal should be granted; and

(E) a copy of the interlocutory order or decree and any related opinion or memorandum.

(2) *Response*. A party may file with the district or BAP clerk a response in opposition or a crossmotion within 14 days after the motion is served.

(c) **Transmitting the Notice of Appeal and the Motion; Docketing the Appeal; Determining the Motion**.

(1) *Transmitting to the District Court or BAP.* The bankruptcy clerk must promptly transmit the notice of appeal and the motion for leave to the BAP clerk if a BAP has been established for appeals from that district and the appellant has not elected to have the district court hear the appeal. Otherwise, the bankruptcy clerk must promptly transmit the notice and motion to the district clerk.

(2) *Docketing in the District Court or BAP.* Upon receiving the notice and motion, the district or BAP clerk must docket the appeal under the title of the bankruptcy case and the title of any adversary proceeding, and must identify the appellant, adding the appellant's name if necessary.

(3) *Oral Argument Not Required.* The motion and any response or cross-motion are submitted without oral argument unless the district court or BAP orders otherwise.

(d) **Failure to File a Motion with a Notice of Appeal**. If an appellant timely files a notice of appeal under this rule but does not include a motion for leave, the district court or BAP may order the appellant to file a motion for leave, or treat the notice of appeal as a motion for leave and either grant or deny it. If the court orders that a motion for leave be filed, the appellant must do so within 14 days after the order is entered, unless the order provides otherwise.

(e) **Direct Appeal to a Court of Appeals**. If leave to appeal an interlocutory order or decree is required under 28 U.S.C. § 158(a)(3), an authorization of a direct appeal by the court of appeals under 28 U.S.C. § 158(d)(2) satisfies the requirement.

Rule 8005. Election to Have an Appeal Heard by the District Court Instead of the BAP

(a) **Filing of a Statement of Election**. To elect to have an appeal heard by the district court, a party must:
(1) file a statement of election that conforms substantially to the appropriate Official Form; and
(2) do so within the time prescribed by 28 U.S.C. § 158(c)(1).

(b) **Transmitting the Documents Related to the Appeal**. Upon receiving an appellant's timely statement of election, the bankruptcy clerk must transmit to the district clerk all documents related to the appeal. Upon receiving a timely statement of election by a party other than the appellant, the BAP clerk must transmit to the district clerk all documents related to the appeal and notify the bankruptcy clerk of the transmission.

(c) **Determining the Validity of an Election**. A party seeking a determination of the validity of an election must file a motion in the court where the appeal is then pending. The motion must be filed within 14 days after the statement of election is filed.

(d) **Motion for Leave without a Notice of Appeal—Effect on the Timing of an Election**. If an appellant moves for leave to appeal under Rule 8004 but fails to file a separate notice of appeal with the motion, the motion must be treated as a notice of appeal for purposes of determining the timeliness of a statement of election.

Rule 8006. Certifying a Direct Appeal to the Court of Appeals

(a) **Effective Date of a Certification**. A certification of a judgment, order, or decree of a bankruptcy court for direct review in a court of appeals under 28 U.S.C. § 158(d)(2) is effective when:

    (1) the certification has been filed;

    (2) a timely appeal has been taken under Rule 8003 or 8004; and

    (3) the notice of appeal has become effective under Rule 8002.

(b) **Filing the Certification**. The certification must be filed with the clerk of the court where the matter is pending. For purposes of this rule, a matter remains pending in the bankruptcy court for 30 days after the effective date under Rule 8002 of the first notice of appeal from the judgment, order, or decree for which direct review is sought. A matter is pending in the district court or BAP thereafter.

(c) **Joint Certification by All Appellants and Appellees**. A joint certification by all the appellants and appellees under 28 U.S.C. § 158(d)(2)(A) must be made by using the appropriate Official Form. The parties may supplement the certification with a short statement of the basis for the certification, which may include the information listed in subdivision (f)(2).

(d) **The Court that May Make the Certification**. Only the court where the matter is pending, as provided in subdivision (b), may certify a direct review on request of parties or on its own motion.

(e) **Certification on the Court's Own Motion**.

    (1) How Accomplished. A certification on the court's own motion must be set forth in a separate document. The clerk of the certifying court must serve it on the parties to the appeal in the manner required for service of a notice of appeal under Rule 8003(c)(1). The certification must be accompanied by an opinion or memorandum that contains the information required by subdivision (f)(2)(A)-(D). (2) Supplemental Statement by a Party. Within 14 days after the court's certification, a party may file with the clerk of the certifying court a short supplemental statement regarding the merits of certification.

(f) **Certification by the Court On Request**.

    (1) *How Requested*. A request by a party for certification that a circumstance specified in 28 U.S.C. §158(d)(2)(A)(i)-(iii) applies—or a request by a majority of the appellants and a majority of the appellees—must be filed with the clerk of the court where the matter is pending within 60 days after the entry of the judgment, order, or decree.

    (2) *Service and Contents*. The request must be served on all parties to the appeal in the manner required for service of a notice of appeal under Rule 8003(c)(1), and it must include the following:

        (A) the facts necessary to understand the question presented;

      (B) the question itself;

      (C) the relief sought;

      (D) the reasons why the direct appeal should be allowed, including which circumstance specified in 28 U.S.C. § 158(d)(2)(A)(i)-(iii) applies; and

      (E) a copy of the judgment, order, or decree and any related opinion or memorandum.

    (3) *Time to File a Response or a Cross-Request.* A party may file a response to the request within 14 days after the request is served, or such other time as the court where the matter is pending allows. A party may file a cross-request for certification within 14 days after the request is served, or within 60 days after the entry of the judgment, order, or decree, whichever occurs first.

    (4) *Oral Argument Not Required.* The request, cross-request, and any response are submitted without oral argument unless the court where the matter is pending orders otherwise.

    (5) *Form and Service of the Certification.* If the court certifies a direct appeal in response to the request, it must do so in a separate document. The certification must be served on the parties to the appeal in the manner required for service of a notice of appeal under Rule 8003(c)(1).

(g) **Proceeding in the Court of Appeals Following a Certification.** Within 30 days after the date the certification becomes effective under subdivision (a), a request for permission to take a direct appeal to the court of appeals must be filed with the circuit clerk in accordance with F.R.App.P. 6(c).

Rule 8007. Stay Pending Appeal; Bonds; Suspension of Proceedings

(a) **Initial Motion in the Bankruptcy Court.**

    (1) *In General.* Ordinarily, a party must move first in the bankruptcy court for the following relief:

      (A) a stay of a judgment, order, or decree of the bankruptcy court pending appeal;

      (B) the approval of a supersedeas bond;

      (C) an order suspending, modifying, restoring, or granting an injunction while an appeal is pending; or

      (D) the suspension or continuation of proceedings in a case or other relief permitted by subdivision (e).

    (2) *Time to File.* The motion may be made either before or after the notice of appeal is filed.

(b) **Motion in the District Court, the BAP, or the Court of Appeals on Direct Appeal.**

    (1) *Request for Relief.* A motion for the relief specified in subdivision (a)(1)—or to vacate or modify a bankruptcy court's order granting such relief—may be made in the court where the appeal is pending.

(2) *Showing or Statement Required.* The motion must:
   (A) show that moving first in the bankruptcy court would be impracticable; or
   (B) if a motion was made in the bankruptcy court, either state that the court has not yet ruled on the motion, or state that the court has ruled and set out any reasons given for the ruling.

(3) *Additional Content.* The motion must also include:
   (A) the reasons for granting the relief requested and the facts relied upon;
   (B) affidavits or other sworn statements supporting facts subject to dispute; and
   (C) relevant parts of the record.

(4) Serving Notice. The movant must give reasonable notice of the motion to all parties.

(c) **Filing a Bond or Other Security**. The district court, BAP, or court of appeals may condition relief on filing a bond or other appropriate security with the bankruptcy court.

(d) **Bond for a Trustee or the United States**. The court may require a trustee to file a bond or other appropriate security when the trustee appeals. A bond or other security is not required when an appeal is taken by the United States, its officer, or its agency or by direction of any department of the federal government.

(e) **Continuation of Proceedings in the Bankruptcy Court**. Despite Rule 7062 and subject to the authority of the district court, BAP, or court of appeals, the bankruptcy court may:
   (1) suspend or order the continuation of other proceedings in the case; or
   (2) issue any other appropriate orders during the pendency of an appeal to protect the rights of all parties in interest.

Rule 8008. Indicative Rulings

(a) **Relief Pending Appeal**. If a party files a timely motion in the bankruptcy court for relief that the court lacks authority to grant because of an appeal that has been docketed and is pending, the bankruptcy court may:
   (1) defer considering the motion;
   (2) deny the motion; or
   (3) state that the court would grant the motion if the court where the appeal is pending remands for that purpose, or state that the motion raises a substantial issue.

(b) **Notice to the Court where the Appeal Is Pending**. The movant must promptly notify the clerk of the court where the appeal is pending if the bankruptcy court states that it would grant the motion or that the motion raises a substantial issue.

(c) **Remand after an Indicative Ruling**. If the bankruptcy court states that it would grant the motion or that the motion raises a substantial issue, the district court or BAP may remand for further proceedings, but it retains jurisdiction unless it expressly dismisses the appeal. If the district court or

BAP remands but retains jurisdiction, the parties must promptly notify the clerk of that court when the bankruptcy court has decided the motion on remand.

Rule 8009. Record on Appeal; Sealed Documents

(a) **Designating the Record on Appeal; Statement of the Issues.**

   (1) *Appellant.*

      (A) The appellant must file with the bankruptcy clerk and serve on the appellee a designation of the items to be included in the record on appeal and a statement of the issues to be presented.

      (B) The appellant must file and serve the designation and statement within 14 days after:

         (i) the appellant's notice of appeal as of right becomes effective under Rule 8002; or

         (ii) an order granting leave to appeal is entered.

      A designation and statement served prematurely must be treated as served on the first day on which filing is timely.

   (2) *Appellee and Cross-Appellant.* Within 14 days after being served, the appellee may file with the bankruptcy clerk and serve on the appellant a designation of additional items to be included in the record. An appellee who files a cross-appeal must file and serve a designation of additional items to be included in the record and a statement of the issues to be presented on the cross-appeal.

   (3) *Cross-Appellee.* Within 14 days after service of the cross-appellant's designation and statement, a cross-appellee may file with the bankruptcy clerk and serve on the cross-appellant a designation of additional items to be included in the record.

   (4) *Record on Appeal.* The record on appeal must include the following:

- docket entries kept by the bankruptcy clerk;
- items designated by the parties;
- the notice of appeal;
- the judgment, order, or decree being appealed;
- any order granting leave to appeal;
- any certification required for a direct appeal to the court of appeals;
- any opinion, findings of fact, and conclusions of law relating to the issues on appeal, including transcripts of all oral rulings;
- any transcript ordered under subdivision (b);
- any statement required by subdivision (c); and . any additional items from the record that the court where the appeal is pending orders.

   (5) *Copies for the Bankruptcy Clerk.* If paper copies are needed, a party filing a designation of items must provide a copy of any of those items that the bankruptcy clerk requests. If the party fails to do so, the bankruptcy clerk must prepare the copy at the party's expense.

(b) **Transcript of Proceedings.**

(1) *Appellant's Duty to Order.* Within the time period prescribed by subdivision (a)(1), the appellant must:
   (A) order in writing from the reporter, as defined in Rule 8010(a)(1), a transcript of such parts of the proceedings not already on file as the appellant considers necessary for the appeal, and file a copy of the order with the bankruptcy clerk; or
   (B) file with the bankruptcy clerk a certificate stating that the appellant is not ordering a transcript.

(2) *Cross-Appellant's Duty to Order.* Within 14 days after the appellant files a copy of the transcript order or a certificate of not ordering a transcript, the appellee as cross-appellant must:
   (A) order in writing from the reporter, as defined in Rule 8010(a)(1), a transcript of such additional parts of the proceedings as the crossappellant considers necessary for the appeal, and file a copy of the order with the bankruptcy clerk; or
   (B) file with the bankruptcy clerk a certificate stating that the cross-appellant is not ordering a transcript.

(3) *Appellee's or Cross-Appellee's Right to Order.* Within 14 days after the appellant or crossappellant files a copy of a transcript order or certificate of not ordering a transcript, the appellee or cross-appellee may order in writing from the reporter a transcript of such additional parts of the proceedings as the appellee or cross-appellee considers necessary for the appeal. A copy of the order must be filed with the bankruptcy clerk.

(4) *Payment.* At the time of ordering, a party must make satisfactory arrangements with the reporter for paying the cost of the transcript.

(5) *Unsupported Finding or Conclusion.* If the appellant intends to argue on appeal that a finding or conclusion is unsupported by the evidence or is contrary to the evidence, the appellant must include in the record a transcript of all relevant testimony and copies of all relevant exhibits.

(c) **Statement of the Evidence when a Transcript Is Unavailable**. If a transcript of a hearing or trial is unavailable, the appellant may prepare a statement of the evidence or proceedings from the best available means, including the appellant's recollection. The statement must be filed within the time prescribed by subdivision (a)(1) and served on the appellee, who may serve objections or proposed amendments within 14 days after being served. The statement and any objections or proposed amendments must then be submitted to the bankruptcy court for settlement and approval. As settled and approved, the statement must be included by the bankruptcy clerk in the record on appeal.

(d) **Agreed Statement as the Record on Appeal**. Instead of the record on appeal as defined in subdivision (a), the parties may prepare, sign, and submit to the bankruptcy court a statement of the case showing how the issues presented by the appeal arose and were decided in the bankruptcy court. The statement must set forth only those facts alleged and proved or sought to be proved that are essential to the court's resolution of the issues. If the statement is accurate, it—together with any additions that the bankruptcy court may consider necessary to a full presentation of the issues on appeal—must be approved by the bankruptcy court and must then be certified to the court where the appeal is pending as the record on appeal. The bankruptcy clerk must then transmit it to the clerk of that court within the time provided by Rule 8010. A copy of the agreed statement may be filed in place of the appendix required by Rule 8018(b) or, in the case of a direct appeal to the court of appeals, by F. R. App. P. 30.

(e) **Correcting or Modifying the Record.**

(1) *Submitting to the Bankruptcy Court.* If any difference arises about whether the record accurately discloses what occurred in the bankruptcy court, the difference must be submitted to and settled by the bankruptcy court and the record conformed accordingly. If an item has been improperly designated as part of the record on appeal, a party may move to strike that item.

(2) *Correcting in Other Ways.* If anything material to either party is omitted from or misstated in the record by error or accident, the omission or misstatement may be corrected, and a supplemental record may be certified and transmitted:

(A) on stipulation of the parties;

(B) by the bankruptcy court before or after the record has been forwarded; or

(C) by the court where the appeal is pending.

(3) *Remaining Questions.* All other questions as to the form and content of the record must be presented to the court where the appeal is pending.

(f) **Sealed Documents.** A document placed under seal by the bankruptcy court may be designated as part of the record on appeal. In doing so, a party must identify it without revealing confidential or secret information, but the bankruptcy clerk must not transmit it to the clerk of the court where the appeal is pending as part of the record. Instead, a party must file a motion with the court where the appeal is pending to accept the document under seal. If the motion is granted, the movant must notify the bankruptcy court of the ruling, and the bankruptcy clerk must promptly transmit the sealed document to the clerk of the court where the appeal is pending.

(g) **Other Necessary Actions.** All parties to an appeal must take any other action necessary to enable the bankruptcy clerk to assemble and transmit the record.

Rule 8010. Completing and Transmitting the Record

(a) **Reporter's Duties**.

(1) *Proceedings Recorded Without a Reporter Present.* If proceedings were recorded without a reporter being present, the person or service

selected under bankruptcy court procedures to transcribe the
recording is the reporter for purposes of this rule.

(2) *Preparing and Filing the Transcript.* The reporter must prepare and
file a transcript as follows:

(A) Upon receiving an order for a transcript in accordance with Rule
8009(b), the reporter must file in the bankruptcy court an
acknowledgment of the request that shows when it was received,
and when the reporter expects to have the transcript completed.

(B) After completing the transcript, the reporter must file it with the
bankruptcy clerk, who will notify the district, BAP, or circuit
clerk of its filing.

(C) If the transcript cannot be completed within 30 days after
receiving the order, the reporter must request an extension of
time from the bankruptcy clerk. The clerk must enter on the
docket and notify the parties whether the extension is granted.

(D) If the reporter does not file the transcript on time, the bankruptcy
clerk must notify the bankruptcy judge.

(b) **Clerk's Duties.**

(1) *Transmitting the Record—In General.* Subject to Rule 8009(f) and
subdivision (b)(5) of this rule, when the record is complete, the
bankruptcy clerk must transmit to the clerk of the court where the
appeal is pending either the record or a notice that the record is
available electronically.

(2) *Multiple Appeals.* If there are multiple appeals from a judgment,
order, or decree, the bankruptcy clerk must transmit a single record.

(3) *Receiving the Record.* Upon receiving the record or notice that it is
available electronically, the district, BAP, or circuit clerk must enter
that information on the docket and promptly notify all parties to the
appeal.

(4) *If Paper Copies Are Ordered.* If the court where the appeal is pending
directs that paper copies of the record be provided, the clerk of that
court must so notify the appellant. If the appellant fails to provide
them, the bankruptcy clerk must prepare them at the appellant's
expense.

(5) *When Leave to Appeal is Requested.* Subject to subdivision (c), if a
motion for leave to appeal has been filed under Rule 8004, the
bankruptcy clerk must prepare and transmit the record only after the
district court, BAP, or court of appeals grants leave.

(c) **Record for a Preliminary Motion in the District Court, BAP, or Court
of Appeals.** This subdivision (c) applies if, before the record is
transmitted, a party moves in the district court, BAP, or court of appeals
for any of the following relief:

- leave to appeal;
- dismissal;
- a stay pending appeal;
- approval of a supersedeas bond, or additional security on a bond
or undertaking on appeal; or

- any other intermediate order.

The bankruptcy clerk must then transmit to the clerk of the court where the relief is sought any parts of the record designated by a party to the appeal or a notice that those parts are available electronically.

Rule 8011. Filing and Service; Signature

(a) **Filing**.
  (1) *With the Clerk.* A document required or permitted to be filed in a district court or BAP must be filed with the clerk of that court.
  (2) *Method and Timeliness.*
    (A) In General. Filing may be accomplished by transmission to the clerk of the district court or BAP. Except as provided in subdivision (a)(2)(B) and (C), filing is timely only if the clerk receives the document within the time fixed for filing.
    (B) Brief or Appendix. A brief or appendix is also timely filed if, on or before the last day for filing, it is:
      (i)   mailed to the clerk by first-class mail—or other class of mail that is at least as expeditious—postage prepaid, if the district court's or BAP's procedures permit or require a brief or appendix to be filed by mailing; or
      (ii) dispatched to a third-party commercial carrier for delivery within 3 days to the clerk, if the court's procedures so permit or require.
    (C) Inmate Filing. A document filed by an inmate confined in an institution is timely if deposited in the institution's internal mailing system on or before the last day for filing. If the institution has a system designed for legal mail, the inmate must use that system to receive the benefit of this rule. Timely filing may be shown by a declaration in compliance with 28 U.S.C. § 1746 or by a notarized statement, either of which must set forth the date of deposit and state that first-class postage has been prepaid.
    (D) Copies. If a document is filed electronically, no paper copy is required. If a document is filed by mail or delivery to the district court or BAP, no additional copies are required. But the district court or BAP may require by local rule or by order in a particular case the filing or furnishing of a specified number of paper copies.
  (3) *Clerk's Refusal of Documents.* The court's clerk must not refuse to accept for filing any document transmitted for that purpose solely because it is not presented in proper form as required by these rules or by any local rule or practice.
(b) **Service of All Documents Required**. Unless a rule requires service by the clerk, a party must, at or before the time of the filing of a document, serve it on the other parties to the appeal. Service on a party represented by counsel must be made on the party's counsel.

(c) **Manner of Service**.

    (1) *Methods*. Service must be made electronically, unless it is being made by or on an individual who is not represented by counsel or the court's governing rules permit or require service by mail or other means of delivery. Service may be made by or on an unrepresented party by any of the following methods:

        (A) personal delivery;

        (B) mail; or

        (C) third-party commercial carrier for delivery within 3 days.

    (2) *When Service is Complete*. Service by electronic means is complete on transmission, unless the party making service receives notice that the document was not transmitted successfully. Service by mail or by commercial carrier is complete on mailing or delivery to the carrier.

(d) **Proof of Service**.

    (1) *What is Required*. A document presented for filing must contain either:

        (A) an acknowledgment of service by the person served; or

        (B) proof of service consisting of a statement by the person who made service certifying:

            (i)   the date and manner of service;

            (ii) the names of the persons served; and

            (iii) the mail or electronic address, the fax number, or the address of the place of delivery, as appropriate for the manner of service, for each person served.

    (2) *Delayed Proof*. The district or BAP clerk may permit documents to be filed without acknowledgment or proof of service, but must require the acknowledgment or proof to be filed promptly thereafter.

    (3) *Brief or Appendix*. When a brief or appendix is filed, the proof of service must also state the date and manner by which it was filed.

(e) **Signature**. Every document filed electronically must include the electronic signature of the person filing it or, if the person is represented, the electronic signature of counsel. The electronic signature must be provided by electronic means that are consistent with any technical standards that the Judicial Conference of the United States establishes. Every document filed in paper form must be signed by the person filing the document or, if the person is represented, by counsel.

Rule 8012. Corporate Disclosure Statement

(a) Who Must File. Any nongovernmental corporate party appearing in the district court or BAP must file a statement that identifies any parent corporation and any publicly held corporation that owns 10% or more of its stock or states that there is no such corporation.

(b) Time to File; Supplemental Filing. A party must file the statement with its principal brief or upon filing a motion, response, petition, or answer in the district court or BAP, whichever occurs first, unless a local rule requires earlier filing. Even if the statement has already been filed, the party's principal brief must include a statement before the table of contents. A party must supplement its statement whenever the required information changes.

Rule 8013. Motions; Intervention

(a) **Contents of a Motion; Response; Reply.**

    (1) *Request for Relief.* A request for an order or other relief is made by filing a motion with the district or BAP clerk, with proof of service on the other parties to the appeal.

    (2) *Contents of a Motion.*

        (A) Grounds and the Relief Sought. A motion must state with particularity the grounds for the motion, the relief sought, and the legal argument necessary to support it.

        (B) Motion to Expedite an Appeal. A motion to expedite an appeal must explain what justifies considering the appeal ahead of other matters. If the district court or BAP grants the motion, it may accelerate the time to transmit the record, the deadline for filing briefs and other documents, oral argument, and the resolution of the appeal. A motion to expedite an appeal may be filed as an emergency motion under subdivision (d).

        (C) Accompanying Documents.

            (i) Any affidavit or other document necessary to support a motion must be served and filed with the motion.

            (ii) An affidavit must contain only factual information, not legal argument.

            (iii) A motion seeking substantive relief must include a copy of the bankruptcy court's judgment, order, or decree, and any accompanying opinion as a separate exhibit.

        (D) Documents Barred or Not Required.

            (i) A separate brief supporting or responding to a motion must not be filed.

            (ii) Unless the court orders otherwise, a notice of motion or a proposed order is not required.

    (3) *Response and Reply; Time to File.* Unless the district court or BAP orders otherwise,

        (A) any party to the appeal may file a response to the motion within 7 days after service of the motion; and

        (B) the movant may file a reply to a response within 7 days after service of the response, but may only address matters raised in the response.

(b) **Disposition of a Motion for a Procedural Order**. The district court or BAP may rule on a motion for a procedural order—including a motion under Rule 9006(b) or (c)—at any time without awaiting a response. A party adversely affected by the ruling may move to reconsider, vacate, or modify it within 7 days after the procedural order is served.

(c) **Oral Argument**. A motion will be decided without oral argument unless the district court or BAP orders otherwise.

(d) **Emergency Motion.**

(1) *Noting the Emergency*. When a movant requests expedited action on a motion because irreparable harm would occur during the time needed to consider a response, the movant must insert the word "Emergency" before the title of the motion.

(2) *Contents of the Motion*. The emergency motion must

(A) be accompanied by an affidavit setting out the nature of the emergency;

(B) state whether all grounds for it were submitted to the bankruptcy court and, if not, why the motion should not be remanded for the bankruptcy court to consider;

(C) include the e-mail addresses, office addresses, and telephone numbers of moving counsel and, when known, of opposing counsel and any unrepresented parties to the appeal; and

(D) be served as prescribed by Rule 8011.

(3) *Notifying Opposing Parties*. Before filing an emergency motion, the movant must make every practicable effort to notify opposing counsel and any unrepresented parties in time for them to respond. The affidavit accompanying the emergency motion must state when and how notice was given or state why giving it was impracticable.

(e) **Power of a Single Bap Judge to Entertain a Motion.**

(1) *Single Judge's Authority*. A BAP judge may act alone on any motion, but may not dismiss or otherwise determine an appeal, deny a motion for leave to appeal, or deny a motion for a stay pending appeal if denial would make the appeal moot.

(2) *Reviewing a Single Judge's Action*. The BAP may review a single judge's action, either on its own motion or on a party's motion.

(f) **Form of Documents; Page Limits; Number of Copies**.

(1) *Format of a Paper Document*. Rule 27(d)(1) F. R. App. P. applies in the district court or BAP to a paper version of a motion, response, or reply.

(2) *Format of an Electronically Filed Document*. A motion, response, or reply filed electronically must comply with the requirements for a paper version regarding covers, line spacing, margins, typeface, and type style. It must also comply with the page limits under paragraph (3).

(3) *Page Limits*. Unless the district court or BAP orders otherwise:

(A) a motion or a response to a motion must not exceed 20 pages, exclusive of the corporate disclosure statement and accompanying documents authorized by subdivision (a)(2)(C); and

(B) a reply to a response must not exceed 10 pages.

(4) *Paper Copies*. Paper copies must be provided only if required by local rule or by an order in a particular case.

(g) **Intervening in an Appeal**. Unless a statute provides otherwise, an entity that seeks to intervene in an appeal pending in the district court or BAP must move for leave to intervene and serve a copy of the motion on the parties to the appeal. The motion or other notice of intervention authorized by statute must be filed within 30 days after the appeal is docketed. It must concisely state the movant's interest, the grounds for intervention, whether intervention was sought in the bankruptcy court, why intervention is being sought at this stage of the proceeding, and why participating as an amicus curiae would not be adequate.

Rule 8014. Briefs

(a) **Appellant's Brief**. The appellant's brief must contain the following under appropriate headings and in the order indicated:
   (1) a corporate disclosure statement, if required by Rule 8012;
   (2) a table of contents, with page references;
   (3) a table of authorities—cases (alphabetically arranged), statutes, and other authorities—with references to the pages of the brief where they are cited;
   (4) a jurisdictional statement, including:
      (A) the basis for the bankruptcy court's subject-matter jurisdiction, with citations to applicable statutory provisions and stating relevant facts establishing jurisdiction;
      (B) the basis for the district court's or BAP's jurisdiction, with citations to applicable statutory provisions and stating relevant facts establishing jurisdiction;
      (C) the filing dates establishing the timeliness of the appeal; and
      (D) an assertion that the appeal is from a final judgment, order, or decree, or information establishing the district court's or BAP's jurisdiction on another basis;
   (5) a statement of the issues presented and, for each one, a concise statement of the applicable standard of appellate review;
   (6) a concise statement of the case setting out the facts relevant to the issues submitted for review, describing the relevant procedural history, and identifying the rulings presented for review, with appropriate references to the record;
   (7) a summary of the argument, which must contain a succinct, clear, and accurate statement of the arguments made in the body of the brief, and which must not merely repeat the argument headings;
   (8) the argument, which must contain the appellant's contentions and the reasons for them, with citations to the authorities and parts of the record on which the appellant relies;
   (9) a short conclusion stating the precise relief sought; and
   (10) the certificate of compliance, if required by Rule 8015(a)(7) or (b).
(b) **Appellee's Brief**. The appellee's brief must conform to the requirements of subdivision (a)(1)-(8) and (10), except that none of the following need appear unless the appellee is dissatisfied with the appellant's statement:

(1) the jurisdictional statement;

(2) the statement of the issues and the applicable standard of appellate review; and

(3) the statement of the case.

(c) **Reply Brief**. The appellant may file a brief in reply to the appellee's brief. A reply brief must comply with the requirements of subdivision (a)(2)-(3).

(d) **Statutes, Rules, Regulations, or Similar Authority**. If the court's determination of the issues presented requires the study of the Code or other statutes, rules, regulations, or similar authority, the relevant parts must be set out in the brief or in an addendum.

(e) **Briefs in a Case Involving Multiple Appellants or Appellees**. In a case involving more than one appellant or appellee, including consolidated cases, any number of appellants or appellees may join in a brief, and any party may adopt by reference a part of another's brief. Parties may also join in reply briefs.

(f) **Citation of Supplemental Authorities**. If pertinent and significant authorities come to a party's attention after the party's brief has been filed—or after oral argument but before a decision—a party may promptly advise the district or BAP clerk by a signed submission setting forth the citations. The submission, which must be served on the other parties to the appeal, must state the reasons for the supplemental citations, referring either to the pertinent page of a brief or to a point argued orally. The body of the submission must not exceed 350 words. Any response must be made within 7 days after the party is served, unless the court orders otherwise, and must be similarly limited.

Rule 8015. Form and Length of Briefs; Form of Appendices and Other Papers

(a) **Paper Copies of a Brief**. If a paper copy of a brief may or must be filed, the following provisions apply:

(1) *Reproduction.*

    (A) A brief may be reproduced by any process that yields a clear black image on light paper. The paper must be opaque and unglazed. Only one side of the paper may be used.

    (B) Text must be reproduced with a clarity that equals or exceeds the output of a laser printer.

    (C) Photographs, illustrations, and tables may be reproduced by any method that results in a good copy of the original. A glossy finish is acceptable if the original is glossy.

(2) *Cover.* The front cover of a brief must contain:

    (A) the number of the case centered at the top;

    (B) the name of the court;

    (C) the title of the case as prescribed by Rule 8003(d)(2) or 8004(c)(2);

    (D) the nature of the proceeding and the name of the court below;

(E) the title of the brief, identifying the party or parties for whom the brief is filed; and

(F) the name, office address, telephone number, and e-mail address of counsel representing the party for whom the brief is filed.

(3) *Binding.* The brief must be bound in any manner that is secure, does not obscure the text, and permits the brief to lie reasonably flat when open.

(4) *Paper Size, Line Spacing, and Margins.* The brief must be on 8½-by-11 inch paper. The text must be double-spaced, but quotations more than two lines long may be indented and single-spaced. Headings and footnotes may be single-spaced. Margins must be at least one inch on all four sides. Page numbers may be placed in the margins, but no text may appear there.

(5) *Typeface.* Either a proportionally spaced or monospaced face may be used.

(A) A proportionally spaced face must include serifs, but sans-serif type may be used in headings and captions. A proportionally spaced face must be 14-point or larger.

(B) A monospaced face may not contain more than 10½ characters per inch.

(6) *Type Styles.* A brief must be set in plain, roman style, although italics or boldface may be used for emphasis. Case names must be italicized or underlined.

(7) *Length.*

(A) Page limitation. A principal brief must not exceed 30 pages, or a reply brief 15 pages, unless it complies with (B) and (C).

(B) Type-volume limitation.

(i) A principal brief is acceptable if:
- it contains no more than 14,000 words; or
- it uses a monospaced face and contains no more than 1,300 lines of text.

(ii) A reply brief is acceptable if it contains no more than half of the type volume specified in item (i).

(iii) Headings, footnotes, and quotations count toward the word and line limitations. The corporate disclosure statement, table of contents, table of citations, statement with respect to oral argument, any addendum containing statutes, rules, or regulations, and any certificates of counsel do not count toward the limitation.

(C) Certificate of Compliance.

(i) A brief submitted under subdivision (a)(7)(B) must include a certificate signed by the attorney, or an unrepresented party, that the brief complies with the type-volume limitation. The person preparing the certificate may rely on the word or line count of the wordprocessing system used to prepare the brief. The certificate must state either:
- the number of words in the brief; or

- • the number of lines of monospaced type in the brief.
(ii) The certification requirement is satisfied by a certificate of compliance that conforms substantially to the appropriate Official Form.
(b) **Electronically Filed Briefs.** A brief filed electronically must comply with subdivision (a), except for (a)(1), (a)(3), and the paper requirement of (a)(4).
(c) **Paper Copies of Appendices.** A paper copy of an appendix must comply with subdivision (a)(1), (2), (3), and (4), with the following exceptions:
  (1) An appendix may include a legible photocopy of any document found in the record or of a printed decision.
  (2) When necessary to facilitate inclusion of odd-sized documents such as technical drawings, an appendix may be a size other than 8½-by-11 inches, and need not lie reasonably flat when opened.
(d) **Electronically Filed Appendices.** An appendix filed electronically must comply with subdivision (a)(2) and (4), except for the paper requirement of (a)(4).
(e) **Other Documents.**
  (1) *Motion.* Rule 8013(f) governs the form of a motion, response, or reply.
  (2) *Paper Copies of Other Documents.* A paper copy of any other document, other than a submission under Rule 8014(f), must comply with subdivision (a), with the following exceptions:
    (A) A cover is not necessary if the caption and signature page together contain the information required by subdivision (a)(2).
    (B) Subdivision (a)(7) does not apply.
  (3) *Other Documents Filed Electronically.* Any other document filed electronically, other than a submission under Rule 8014(f), must comply with the appearance requirements of paragraph (2).
(f) **Local Variation.** A district court or BAP must accept documents that comply with the applicable requirements of this rule. By local rule, a district court or BAP may accept documents that do not meet all of the requirements of this rule.

Rule 8016. Cross-Appeals

(a) **Applicability.** This rule applies to a case in which a cross-appeal is filed. Rules 8014(a)-(c), 8015(a)(7)(A)-(B), and 8018(a)(1)-(3) do not apply to such a case, except as otherwise provided in this rule.
(b) **Designation of Appellant.** The party who files a notice of appeal first is the appellant for purposes of this rule and Rule 8018(a)(4) and (b) and Rule 8019. If notices are filed on the same day, the plaintiff, petitioner, applicant, or movant in the proceeding below is the appellant. These designations may be modified by the parties' agreement or by court order.
(c) **Briefs.** In a case involving a cross-appeal:
  (1) *Appellant's Principal Brief.* The appellant must file a principal brief in the appeal. That brief must comply with Rule 8014(a).

(2) *Appellee's Principal and Response Brief.* The appellee must file a principal brief in the crossappeal and must, in the same brief, respond to the principal brief in the appeal. That brief must comply with Rule 8014(a), except that the brief need not include a statement of the case unless the appellee is dissatisfied with the appellant's statement.

(3) *Appellant's Response and Reply Brief.* The appellant must file a brief that responds to the principal brief in the cross-appeal and may, in the same brief, reply to the response in the appeal. That brief must comply with Rule 8014(a)(2)-(8) and (10), except that none of the following need appear unless the appellant is dissatisfied with the appellee's statement in the cross-appeal:

(A) the jurisdictional statement;

(B) the statement of the issues and the applicable standard of appellate review; and

(C) the statement of the case.

(4) *Appellee's Reply Brief.* The appellee may file a brief in reply to the response in the cross-appeal. That brief must comply with Rule 8014(a)(2)-(3) and (10) and must be limited to the issues presented by the cross-appeal.

(d) **Length.**

(1) *Page Limitation.* Unless it complies with paragraphs (2) and (3), the appellant's principal brief must not exceed 30 pages; the appellee's principal and response brief, 35 pages; the appellant's response and reply brief, 30 pages; and the appellee's reply brief, 15 pages.

(2) *Type-Volume Limitation.*

(A) The appellant's principal brief or the appellant's response and reply brief is acceptable if:

(i) it contains no more than 14,000 words; or

(ii) it uses a monospaced face and contains no more than 1,300 lines of text.

(B) The appellee's principal and response brief is acceptable if:

(i) it contains no more than 16,500 words; or

(ii) it uses a monospaced face and contains no more than 1,500 lines of text.

(C) The appellee's reply brief is acceptable if it contains no more than half of the type volume specified in subparagraph (A).

(D) Headings, footnotes, and quotations count toward the word and line limitations. The corporate disclosure statement, table of contents, table of citations, statement with respect to oral argument, any addendum containing statutes, rules, or regulations, and any certificates of counsel do not count toward the limitation.

(3) *Certificate of Compliance.* A brief submitted either electronically or in paper form under paragraph (2) must comply with Rule 8015(a)(7)(C).

(e) **Time to Serve and File a Brief**. Briefs must be served and filed as follows, unless the district court or BAP by order in a particular case excuses the filing of briefs or specifies different time limits:

    (1) the appellant's principal brief, within 30 days after the docketing of notice that the record has been transmitted or is available electronically;

    (2) the appellee's principal and response brief, within 30 days after the appellant's principal brief is served;

    (3) the appellant's response and reply brief, within 30 days after the appellee's principal and response brief is served; and

    (4) the appellee's reply brief, within 14 days after the appellant's response and reply brief is served, but at least 7 days before scheduled argument unless the district court or BAP, for good cause, allows a later filing.

Rule 8017. Brief of an Amicus Curiae

(a) **When Permitted**. The United States or its officer or agency or a state may file an amicus-curiae brief without the consent of the parties or leave of court. Any other amicus curiae may file a brief only by leave of court or if the brief states that all parties have consented to its filing. On its own motion, and with notice to all parties to an appeal, the district court or BAP may request a brief by an amicus curiae.

(b) **Motion for Leave to File**. The motion must be accompanied by the proposed brief and state:

    (1) the movant's interest; and

    (2) the reason why an amicus brief is desirable and why the matters asserted are relevant to the disposition of the appeal.

(c) **Contents and Form**. An amicus brief must comply with Rule 8015. In addition to the requirements of Rule 8015, the cover must identify the party or parties supported and indicate whether the brief supports affirmance or reversal. If an amicus curiae is a corporation, the brief must include a disclosure statement like that required of parties by Rule 8012. An amicus brief need not comply with Rule 8014, but must include the following:

    (1) a table of contents, with page references;

    (2) a table of authorities-cases (alphabetically arranged), statutes, and other authorities-with references to the pages of the brief where they are cited;

    (3) a concise statement of the identity of the amicus curiae, its interest in the case, and the source of its authority to file;

    (4) unless the amicus curiae is one listed in the first sentence of subdivision (a), a statement that indicates whether:

        (A) a party's counsel authored the brief in whole or in part;

        (B) a party or a party's counsel contributed money that was intended to fund preparing or submitting the brief; and

> (C) a person—other than the amicus curiae, its members, or its counsel—contributed money that was intended to fund preparing or submitting the brief and, if so, identifies each such person;
>
> (5) an argument, which may be preceded by a summary and need not include a statement of the applicable standard of review; and
>
> (6) a certificate of compliance, if required by Rule 8015(a)(7)(C) or 8015(b).

(d) **Length**. Except by the district court's or BAP's permission, an amicus brief must be no more than one-half the maximum length authorized by these rules for a party's principal brief. If the court grants a party permission to file a longer brief, that extension does not affect the length of an amicus brief.

(e) **Time for Filing**. An amicus curiae must file its brief, accompanied by a motion for filing when necessary, no later than 7 days after the principal brief of the party being supported is filed. An amicus curiae that does not support either party must file its brief no later than 7 days after the appellant's principal brief is filed. The district court or BAP may grant leave for later filing, specifying the time within which an opposing party may answer.

(f) **Reply Brief**. Except by the district court's or BAP's permission, an amicus curiae may not file a reply brief.

(g) **Oral Argument**. An amicus curiae may participate in oral argument only with the district court's or BAP's permission.

Rule 8018. Serving and Filing Briefs; Appendices

(a) **Time to Serve and File a Brief**. The following rules apply unless the district court or BAP by order in a particular case excuses the filing of briefs or specifies different time limits:

(1) The appellant must serve and file a brief within 30 days after the docketing of notice that the record has been transmitted or is available electronically.

(2) The appellee must serve and file a brief within 30 days after service of the appellant's brief.

(3) The appellant may serve and file a reply brief within 14 days after service of the appellee's brief, but a reply brief must be filed at least 7 days before scheduled argument unless the district court or BAP, for good cause, allows a later filing.

(4) If an appellant fails to file a brief on time or within an extended time authorized by the district court or BAP, an appellee may move to dismiss the appeal—or the district court or BAP, after notice, may dismiss the appeal on its own motion. An appellee who fails to file a brief will not be heard at oral argument unless the district court or BAP grants permission.

(b) **Duty to Serve and File an Appendix to the Brief.**

(1) *Appellant.* Subject to subdivision (e) and Rule 8009(d), the appellant must serve and file with its principal brief excerpts of the record as an appendix. It must contain the following:
(A) the relevant entries in the bankruptcy docket;
(B) the complaint and answer, or other equivalent filings;
(C) the judgment, order, or decree from which the appeal is taken;
(D) any other orders, pleadings, jury instructions, findings, conclusions, or opinions relevant to the appeal;
(E) the notice of appeal; and
(F) any relevant transcript or portion of it.
(2) *Appellee.* The appellee may also serve and file with its brief an appendix that contains material required to be included by the appellant or relevant to the appeal or cross-appeal, but omitted by the appellant.
(3) *Cross-Appellee.* The appellant as crossappellee may also serve and file with its response an appendix that contains material relevant to matters raised initially by the principal brief in the crossappeal, but omitted by the cross-appellant.
(c) **Format of the Appendix**. The appendix must begin with a table of contents identifying the page at which each part begins. The relevant docket entries must follow the table of contents. Other parts of the record must follow chronologically. When pages from the transcript of proceedings are placed in the appendix, the transcript page numbers must be shown in brackets immediately before the included pages. Omissions in the text of documents or of the transcript must be indicated by asterisks. Immaterial formal matters (captions, subscriptions, acknowledgments, and the like) should be omitted.
(d) **Exhibits**. Exhibits designated for inclusion in the appendix may be reproduced in a separate volume or volumes, suitably indexed.
(e) **Appeal on the Original Record without an Appendix**. The district court or BAP may, either by rule for all cases or classes of cases or by order in a particular case, dispense with the appendix and permit an appeal to proceed on the original record, with the submission of any relevant parts of the record that the district court or BAP orders the parties to file.

Rule 8019. Oral Argument

(a) **Party's Statement**. Any party may file, or a district court or BAP may require, a statement explaining why oral argument should, or need not, be permitted.
(b) **Presumption of Oral Argument and Exceptions**. Oral argument must be allowed in every case unless the district judge—or all the BAP judges assigned to hear the appeal—examine the briefs and record and determine that oral argument is unnecessary because
(1) the appeal is frivolous;
(2) the dispositive issue or issues have been authoritatively decided; or

(3) the facts and legal arguments are adequately presented in the briefs and record, and the decisional process would not be significantly aided by oral argument.

(c) **Notice of Argument; Postponement.** The district court or BAP must advise all parties of the date, time, and place for oral argument, and the time allowed for each side. A motion to postpone the argument or to allow longer argument must be filed reasonably in advance of the hearing date.

(d) **Order and Contents of Argument.** The appellant opens and concludes the argument. Counsel must not read at length from briefs, the record, or authorities.

(e) **Cross-appeals and Separate Appeals.** If there is a cross-appeal, Rule 8016(b) determines which party is the appellant and which is the appellee for the purposes of oral argument. Unless the district court or BAP directs otherwise, a cross-appeal or separate appeal must be argued when the initial appeal is argued. Separate parties should avoid duplicative argument.

(f) **Nonappearance of a Party.** If the appellee fails to appear for argument, the district court or BAP may hear the appellant's argument. If the appellant fails to appear for argument, the district court or BAP may hear the appellee's argument. If neither party appears, the case will be decided on the briefs unless the district court or BAP orders otherwise.

(g) **Submission on Briefs.** The parties may agree to submit a case for decision on the briefs, but the district court or BAP may direct that the case be argued.

(h) **Use of Physical Exhibits at Argument; Removal.** Counsel intending to use physical exhibits other than documents at the argument must arrange to place them in the courtroom on the day of the argument before the court convenes. After the argument, counsel must remove the exhibits from the courtroom unless the district court or BAP directs otherwise. The clerk may destroy or dispose of the exhibits if counsel does not reclaim them within a reasonable time after the clerk gives notice to remove them.

Rule 8020. Frivolous Appeal and Other Misconduct

(a) **Frivolous Appeal—Damages and Costs.** If the district court or BAP determines that an appeal is frivolous, it may, after a separately filed motion or notice from the court and reasonable opportunity to respond, award just damages and single or double costs to the appellee.

(b) **Other Misconduct.** The district court or BAP may discipline or sanction an attorney or party appearing before it for other misconduct, including failure to comply with any court order. First, however, the court must afford the attorney or party reasonable notice, an opportunity to show cause to the contrary, and, if requested, a hearing.

Rule 8021. Costs

(a) **Against Whom Assessed.** The following rules apply unless the law provides or the district court or BAP orders otherwise:

(1) if an appeal is dismissed, costs are taxed against the appellant, unless the parties agree otherwise;

(2) if a judgment, order, or decree is affirmed, costs are taxed against the appellant;

(3) if a judgment, order, or decree is reversed, costs are taxed against the appellee;

(4) if a judgment, order, or decree is affirmed or reversed in part, modified, or vacated, costs are taxed only as the district court or BAP orders.

(b) **Costs for and against the United States.** Costs for or against the United States, its agency, or its officer may be assessed under subdivision (a) only if authorized by law.

(c) **Costs on Appeal Taxable in the Bankruptcy Court.** The following costs on appeal are taxable in the bankruptcy court for the benefit of the party entitled to costs under this rule:

(1) the production of any required copies of a brief, appendix, exhibit, or the record;

(2) the preparation and transmission of the record;

(3) the reporter's transcript, if needed to determine the appeal;

(4) premiums paid for a supersedeas bond or other bonds to preserve rights pending appeal; and

(5) the fee for filing the notice of appeal.

(d) **Bill of Costs; Objections.** A party who wants costs taxed must, within 14 days after entry of judgment on appeal, file with the bankruptcy clerk, with proof of service, an itemized and verified bill of costs. Objections must be filed within 14 days after service of the bill of costs, unless the bankruptcy court extends the time.

Rule 8022. Motion for Rehearing

(a) **Time to File; Contents; Response; Action by the District Court or BAP if Granted**.

(1) *Time.* Unless the time is shortened or extended by order or local rule, any motion for rehearing by the district court or BAP must be filed within 14 days after entry of judgment on appeal.

(2) *Contents.* The motion must state with particularity each point of law or fact that the movant believes the district court or BAP has overlooked or misapprehended and must argue in support of the motion. Oral argument is not permitted.

(3) *Response.* Unless the district court or BAP requests, no response to a motion for rehearing is permitted. But ordinarily, rehearing will not be granted in the absence of such a request.

(4) *Action by the District Court or BAP.* If a motion for rehearing is granted, the district court or BAP may do any of the following:

(A) make a final disposition of the appeal without reargument;

(B) restore the case to the calendar for reargument or resubmission; or

(C) issue any other appropriate order.

(b) **Form of the Motion; Length**. The motion must comply in form with Rule 8013(f)(1) and (2). Copies must be served and filed as provided by Rule 8011. Unless the district court or BAP orders otherwise, a motion for rehearing must not exceed 15 pages.

Rule 8023. Voluntary Dismissal

The clerk of the district court or BAP must dismiss an appeal if the parties file a signed dismissal agreement specifying how costs are to be paid and pay any fees that are due. An appeal may be dismissed on the appellant's motion on terms agreed to by the parties or fixed by the district court or BAP.

Rule 8024. Clerk's Duties on Disposition of the Appeal

(a) **Judgment on Appeal**. The district or BAP clerk must prepare, sign, and enter the judgment after receiving the court's opinion or, if there is no opinion, as the court instructs. Noting the judgment on the docket constitutes entry of judgment.

(b) **Notice of a Judgment**. Immediately upon the entry of a judgment, the district or BAP clerk must:
  (1) transmit a notice of the entry to each party to the appeal, to the United States trustee, and to the bankruptcy clerk, together with a copy of any opinion; and
  (2) note the date of the transmission on the docket.

(c) **Returning Physical Items**. If any physical items were transmitted as the record on appeal, they must be returned to the bankruptcy clerk on disposition of the appeal.

Rule 8025. Stay of a District Court or BAP Judgment

(a) **Automatic Stay of Judgment on Appeal**. Unless the district court or BAP orders otherwise, its judgment is stayed for 14 days after entry.

(b) **Stay Pending Appeal to the Court of Appeals**.
  (1) *In General*. On a party's motion and notice to all other parties to the appeal, the district court or BAP may stay its judgment pending an appeal to the court of appeals.
  (2) *Time Limit*. The stay must not exceed 30 days after the judgment is entered, except for cause shown.
  (3) *Stay Continued*. If, before a stay expires, the party who obtained the stay appeals to the court of appeals, the stay continues until final disposition by the court of appeals.
  (4) *Bond or Other Security*. A bond or other security may be required as a condition for granting or continuing a stay of the judgment. A bond or other security may be required if a trustee obtains a stay, but not if a stay is obtained by the United States or its officer or agency or at the direction of any department of the United States government.

(c) **Automatic Stay of an Order, Judgment, or Decree of a Bankruptcy Court.** If the district court or BAP enters a judgment affirming an order, judgment, or decree of the bankruptcy court, a stay of the district court's or BAP's judgment automatically stays the bankruptcy court's order, judgment, or decree for the duration of the appellate stay.

(d) **Power of a Court of Appeals Not Limited.** This rule does not limit the power of a court of appeals or any of its judges to do the following:

   (1) stay a judgment pending appeal;

   (2) stay proceedings while an appeal is pending;

   (3) suspend, modify, restore, vacate, or grant a stay or an injunction while an appeal is pending; or

   (4) issue any order appropriate to preserve the status quo or the effectiveness of any judgment to be entered.

Rule 8026. Rules by Circuit Councils and District Courts; Procedure When There is No Controlling Law

(a) **Local Rules by Circuit Councils and District Courts.**

   (1) *Adopting Local Rules.* A circuit council that has authorized a BAP under 28 U.S.C. § 158(b) may make and amend rules governing the practice and procedure on appeal from a judgment, order, or decree of a bankruptcy court to the BAP. A district court may make and amend rules governing the practice and procedure on appeal from a judgment, order, or decree of a bankruptcy court to the district court. Local rules must be consistent with, but not duplicative of, Acts of Congress and these Part VIII rules. Rule 83 F.R.Civ.P. governs the procedure for making and amending rules to govern appeals.

   (2) *Numbering.* Local rules must conform to any uniform numbering system prescribed by the Judicial Conference of the United States. (3) Limitation on Imposing Requirements of Form. A local rule imposing a requirement of form must not be enforced in a way that causes a party to lose any right because of a nonwillful failure to comply.

(b) **Procedure when There is No Controlling Law.**

   (1) *In General.* A district court or BAP may regulate practice in any manner consistent with federal law, applicable federal rules, the Official Forms, and local rules.

   (2) *Limitation on Sanctions.* No sanction or other disadvantage may be imposed for noncompliance with any requirement not in federal law, applicable federal rules, the Official Forms, or local rules unless the alleged violator has been furnished in the particular case with actual notice of the requirement.

Rule 8027. Notice of a Mediation Procedure

If the district court or BAP has a mediation procedure applicable to bankruptcy appeals, the clerk must notify the parties promptly after docketing the appeal of:

(a) the requirements of the mediation procedure; and

(b) any effect the mediation procedure has on the time to file briefs.

Rule 8028. Suspension of Rules in Part VIII

In the interest of expediting decision or for other cause in a particular case, the district court or BAP, or where appropriate the court of appeals, may suspend the requirements or provisions of the rules in Part VIII, except Rules 8001, 8002, 8003, 8004, 8005, 8006, 8007, 8012, 8020, 8024, 8025, 8026, and 8028.

Part IX. General provisions

Rule 9001. General Definitions

The definitions of words and phrases in §§ 101, 902, 1101, and 1502 of the Code, and the rules of construction in § 102, govern their use in these rules. In addition, the following words and phrases used in these rules have the meanings indicated:

(1) "Bankruptcy clerk" means a clerk appointed pursuant to 28 U.S.C. § 156(b).

(2) "Bankruptcy Code" or "Code" means title 11 of the United States Code.

(3) "Clerk" means bankruptcy clerk, if one has been appointed, otherwise clerk of the district court.

(4) "Court" or "judge" means the judicial officer before whom a case or proceeding is pending.

(5) "Debtor." When any act is required by these rules to be performed by a debtor or when it is necessary to compel attendance of a debtor for examination and the debtor is not a natural person: (A) if the debtor is a corporation, "debtor" includes, if designated by the court, any or all of its officers, members of its board of directors or trustees or of a similar controlling body, a controlling stockholder or member, or any other person in control; (B) if the debtor is a partnership, "debtor" includes any or all of its general partners or, if designated by the court, any other person in control.

(6) "Firm" includes a partnership or professional corporation of attorneys or accountants.

(7) "Judgment" means any appealable order.

(8) "Mail" means first class, postage prepaid.

(9) "Notice provider" means any entity approved by the Administrative Office of the United States Courts to give notice to creditors under Rule 2002(g)(4).

(10) "Regular associate" means any attorney regularly employed by, associated with, or counsel to an individual or firm.

(11) "Trustee" includes a debtor in possession in a chapter 11 case.

(12) "United States trustee" includes an assistant United States trustee and any designee of the United States trustee.

Rule 9002. Meanings of Words in the Federal Rules of Civil Procedure When Applicable to Cases Under the Code

The following words and phrases used in the Federal Rules of Civil Procedure made applicable to cases under the Code by these rules have the meanings indicated unless they are inconsistent with the context:

(1) "Action" or "civil action" means an adversary proceeding or, when appropriate, a contested petition, or proceedings to vacate an order for relief or to determine any other contested matter.

(2) "Appeal" means an appeal as provided by 28 U.S.C. § 158.

(3) "Clerk" or "clerk of the district court" means the court officer responsible for the bankruptcy records in the district.
(4) "District court," "trial court," "court," "district judge," or "judge" means bankruptcy judge if the case or proceeding is pending before a bankruptcy judge.
(5) "Judgment" includes any order appealable to an appellate court.

Rule 9003. Prohibition of Ex Parte Contacts

(a) **General Prohibition**. Except as otherwise permitted by applicable law, any examiner, any party in interest, and any attorney, accountant, or employee of a party in interest shall refrain from ex parte meetings and communications with the court concerning matters affecting a particular case or proceeding.
(b) **United States Trustee**. Except as otherwise permitted by applicable law, the United States trustee and assistants to and employees or agents of the United States trustee shall refrain from ex parte meetings and communications with the court concerning matters affecting a particular case or proceeding. This rule does not preclude communications with the court to discuss general problems of administration and improvement of bankruptcy administration, including the operation of the United States trustee system.

Rule 9004. General Requirements of Form

(a) **Legibility; Abbreviations**. All petitions, pleadings, schedules and other papers shall be clearly legible. Abbreviations in common use in the English language may be used.
(b) **Caption**. Each paper filed shall contain a caption setting forth the name of the court, the title of the case, the bankruptcy docket number, and a brief designation of the character of the paper.

Rule 9005. Harmless Error

Rule 61 F. R. Civ. P. applies in cases under the Code. When appropriate, the court may order the correction of any error or defect or the cure of any omission which does not affect substantial rights.

Rule 9005.1. Constitutional Challenge to a Statute—Notice, Certification, and Intervention

Rule 5.1 F. R. Civ. P. applies in cases under the Code.

Rule 9006. Computing and Extending Time; Time for Motion Papers

(a) **Computing Time**. The following rules apply in computing any time period specified in these rules, in the Federal Rules of Civil Procedure, in any local rule or court order, or in any statute that does not specify a method of computing time.

(1) *Period Stated in Days or a Longer Unit.* When the period is stated in days or a longer unit of time:

    (A) exclude the day of the event that triggers the period;

    (B) count every day, including intermediate Saturdays, Sundays, and legal holidays; and

    (C) include the last day of the period, but if the last day is a Saturday, Sunday, or legal holiday, the period continues to run until the end of the next day that is not a Saturday, Sunday, or legal holiday.

(2) *Period Stated in Hours.* When the period is stated in hours:

    (A) begin counting immediately on the occurrence of the event that triggers the period;

    (B) count every hour, including hours during intermediate Saturdays, Sundays, and legal holidays; and

    (C) if the period would end on a Saturday, Sunday, or legal holiday, then continue the period until the same time on the next day that is not a Saturday, Sunday, or legal holiday.

(3) *Inaccessibility of Clerk's Office.* Unless the court orders otherwise, if the clerk's office is inaccessible:

    (A) on the last day for filing under Rule 9006(a)(1), then the time for filing is extended to the first accessible day that is not a Saturday, Sunday, or legal holiday; or

    (B) during the last hour for filing under Rule 9006(a)(2), then the time for filing is extended to the same time on the first accessible day that is not a Saturday, Sunday, or legal holiday.

(4) *"Last Day" Defined.* Unless a different time is set by a statute, local rule, or order in the case, the last day ends:

    (A) for electronic filing, at midnight in the court's time zone; and

    (B) for filing by other means, when the clerk's office is scheduled to close.

(5) *"Next Day" Defined.* The "next day" is determined by continuing to count forward when the period is measured after an event and backward when measured before an event.

(6) *"Legal Holiday" Defined.* "Legal holiday" means:

    (A) the day set aside by statute for observing New Year's Day, Martin Luther King Jr.'s Birthday, Washington's Birthday, Memorial Day, Independence Day, Labor Day, Columbus Day, Veterans' Day, Thanksgiving Day, or Christmas Day;

    (B) any day declared a holiday by the President or Congress; and

    (C) for periods that are measured after an event, any other day declared a holiday by the state where the district court is located. (In this rule, "state" includes the District of Columbia and any United States commonwealth or territory.)

(b) **Enlargement.**

(1) *In General.* Except as provided in paragraphs (2) and (3) of this subdivision, when an act is required or allowed to be done at or

within a specified period by these rules or by a notice given thereunder or by order of court, the court for cause shown may at any time in its discretion (1) with or without motion or notice order the period enlarged if the request therefor is made before the expiration of the period originally prescribed or as extended by a previous order or (2) on motion made after the expiration of the specified period permit the act to be done where the failure to act was the result of excusable neglect.

(2) *Enlargement Not Permitted.* The court may not enlarge the time for taking action under Rules 1007(d), 2003(a) and (d), 7052, 9023, and 9024.

(3) *Enlargement Governed by Other Rules.* The court may enlarge the time for taking action under Rules 1006(b)(2), 1017(e), 3002(c), 4003(b), 4004(a), 4007(c), 4008(a), 8002, and 9033, only to the extent and under the conditions stated in those rules. In addition, the court may enlarge the time to file the statement required under Rule 1007(b)(7), and to file schedules and statements in a small business case under § 1116(3) of the Code, only to the extent and under the conditions stated in Rule 1007(c).

(c) **Reduction.**

(1) *In General.* Except as provided in paragraph (2) of this subdivision, when an act is required or allowed to be done at or within a specified time by these rules or by a notice given thereunder or by order of court, the court for cause shown may in its discretion with or without motion or notice order the period reduced.

(2) *Reduction Not Permitted.* The court may not reduce the time for taking action under Rules 2002(a)(7), 2003(a), 3002(c), 3014, 3015, 4001(b)(2), (c)(2), 4003(a), 4004(a), 4007(c), 4008(a), 8002, and 9033(b). In addition, the court may not reduce the time under Rule 1007(c) to file the statement required by Rule 1007(b)(7).

(d) **Motion Papers.** A written motion, other than one which may be heard ex parte, and notice of any hearing shall be served not later than seven days before the time specified for such hearing, unless a different period is fixed by these rules or by order of the court. Such an order may for cause shown be made on ex parte application. When a motion is supported by affidavit, the affidavit shall be served with the motion. Except as otherwise provided in Rule 9023, any written response shall be served not later than one day before the hearing, unless the court permits otherwise.

(e) **Time of Service.** Service of process and service of any paper other than process or of notice by mail is complete on mailing.

(f) **Additional Time After Service by Mail or Under Rule 5(b)(2)(D) or (F) F. R. Civ. P.** When there is a right or requirement to act or undertake some proceedings within a prescribed period after being served and that service is by mail or under Rule 5(b)(2)(D) (leaving with the clerk) or (F) (other means consented to) F. R. Civ. P., three days are added after the prescribed period would otherwise expire under Rule 9006(a).

(g) **Grain Storage Facility Cases**. This rule shall not limit the court's authority under § 557 of the Code to enter orders governing procedures in cases in which the debtor is an owner or operator of a grain storage facility.

Rule 9007. General Authority to Regulate Notices

When notice is to be given under these rules, the court shall designate, if not otherwise specified herein, the time within which, the entities to whom, and the form and manner in which the notice shall be given. When feasible, the court may order any notices under these rules to be combined.

Rule 9008. Service or Notice by Publication

Whenever these rules require or authorize service or notice by publication, the court shall, to the extent not otherwise specified in these rules, determine the form and manner thereof, including the newspaper or other medium to be used and the number of publications.

Rule 9009. Forms

(a) **Official Forms**. The Official Forms prescribed by the Judicial Conference of the United States shall be used without alteration, except as otherwise provided in these rules, in a particular Official Form, or in the national instructions for a particular Official Form. Official Forms may be modified to permit minor changes not affecting wording or the order of presenting information, including changes that:
    (1) expand the prescribed areas for responses in order to permit complete responses;
    (2) delete space not needed for responses; or
    (3) delete items requiring detail in a question or category if the filer indicates—either by checking "no" or "none" or by stating in words—that there is nothing to report on that question or category.
(b) **Director's Forms**. The Director of the Administrative Office of the United States Courts may issue additional forms for use under the Code.
(c) **Construction**. The forms shall be construed to be consistent with these rules and the Code.

Rule 9010. Representation and Appearances; Powers of Attorney

(a) **Authority to Act Personally or by Attorney**. A debtor, creditor, equity security holder, indenture trustee, committee or other party may (1) appear in a case under the Code and act either in the entity's own behalf or by an attorney authorized to practice in the court, and (2) perform any act not constituting the practice of law, by an authorized agent, attorney in fact, or proxy.
(b) **Notice of Appearance**. An attorney appearing for a party in a case under the Code shall file a notice of appearance with the attorney's name, office

address and telephone number, unless the attorney's appearance is otherwise noted in the record.

(c) **Power of Attorney.** The authority of any agent, attorney in fact, or proxy to represent a creditor for any purpose other than the execution and filing of a proof of claim or the acceptance or rejection of a plan shall be evidenced by a power of attorney conforming substantially to the appropriate Official Form. The execution of any such power of attorney shall be acknowledged before one of the officers enumerated in 28 U.S.C. § 459, § 953, Rule 9012, or a person authorized to administer oaths under the laws of the state where the oath is administered.

Rule 9011. Signing of Papers; Representations to the Court; Sanctions; Verification and Copies of Papers

(a) **Signature.** Every petition, pleading, written motion, and other paper, except a list, schedule, or statement, or amendments thereto, shall be signed by at least one attorney of record in the attorney's individual name. A party who is not represented by an attorney shall sign all papers. Each paper shall state the signer's address and telephone number, if any. An unsigned paper shall be stricken unless omission of the signature is corrected promptly after being called to the attention of the attorney or party.

(b) **Representations to the Court.** By presenting to the court (whether by signing, filing, submitting, or later advocating) a petition, pleading, written motion, or other paper, an attorney or unrepresented party is certifying that to the best of the person's knowledge, information, and belief, formed after an inquiry reasonable under the circumstances, —

(1) it is not being presented for any improper purpose, such as to harass or to cause unnecessary delay or needless increase in the cost of litigation;

(2) the claims, defenses, and other legal contentions therein are warranted by existing law or by a nonfrivolous argument for the extension, modification, or reversal of existing law or the establishment of new law;

(3) the allegations and other factual contentions have evidentiary support or, if specifically so identified, are likely to have evidentiary support after a reasonable opportunity for further investigation or discovery; and

(4) the denials of factual contentions are warranted on the evidence or, if specifically so identified, are reasonably based on a lack of information or belief.

(c) **Sanctions.** If, after notice and a reasonable opportunity to respond, the court determines that subdivision (b) has been violated, the court may, subject to the conditions stated below, impose an appropriate sanction upon the attorneys, law firms, or parties that have violated subdivision (b) or are responsible for the violation.

(1) *How Initiated.*
- (A) By Motion. A motion for sanctions under this rule shall be made separately from other motions or requests and shall describe the specific conduct alleged to violate subdivision (b). It shall be served as provided in Rule 7004. The motion for sanctions may not be filed with or presented to the court unless, within 21 days after service of the motion (or such other period as the court may prescribe), the challenged paper, claim, defense, contention, allegation, or denial is not withdrawn or appropriately corrected, except that this limitation shall not apply if the conduct alleged is the filing of a petition in violation of subdivision (b). If warranted, the court may award to the party prevailing on the motion the reasonable expenses and attorney's fees incurred in presenting or opposing the motion. Absent exceptional circumstances, a law firm shall be held jointly responsible for violations committed by its partners, associates, and employees.
- (B) On Court's Initiative. On its own initiative, the court may enter an order describing the specific conduct that appears to violate subdivision (b) and directing an attorney, law firm, or party to show cause why it has not violated subdivision (b) with respect thereto.

(2) *Nature of Sanction; Limitations.* A sanction imposed for violation of this rule shall be limited to what is sufficient to deter repetition of such conduct or comparable conduct by others similarly situated. Subject to the limitations in subparagraphs (A) and (B), the sanction may consist of, or include, directives of a nonmonetary nature, an order to pay a penalty into court, or, if imposed on motion and warranted for effective deterrence, an order directing payment to the movant of some or all of the reasonable attorneys' fees and other expenses incurred as a direct result of the violation.
- (A) Monetary sanctions may not be awarded against a represented party for a violation of subdivision (b)(2).
- (B) Monetary sanctions may not be awarded on the court's initiative unless the court issues its order to show cause before a voluntary dismissal or settlement of the claims made by or against the party which is, or whose attorneys are, to be sanctioned.

(3) *Order.* When imposing sanctions, the court shall describe the conduct determined to constitute a violation of this rule and explain the basis for the sanction imposed.

(d) **Inapplicability to Discovery.** Subdivisions (a) through (c) of this rule do not apply to disclosures and discovery requests, responses, objections, and motions that are subject to the provisions of Rules 7026 through 7037.

(e) **Verification.** Except as otherwise specifically provided by these rules, papers filed in a case under the Code need not be verified. Whenever verification is required by these rules, an unsworn declaration as provided in 28 U.S.C. § 1746satisfies the requirement of verification.

(f) **Copies of Signed or Verified Papers**. When these rules require copies of a signed or verified paper, it shall suffice if the original is signed or verified and the copies are conformed to the original.

Rule 9012. Oaths and Affirmations

(a) **Persons Authorized to Administer Oaths**. The following persons may administer oaths and affirmations and take acknowledgments: a bankruptcy judge, clerk, deputy clerk, United States trustee, officer authorized to administer oaths in proceedings before the courts of the United States or under the laws of the state where the oath is to be taken, or a diplomatic or consular officer of the United States in any foreign country.

(b) **Affirmation in Lieu of Oath**. When in a case under the Code an oath is required to be taken, a solemn affirmation may be accepted in lieu thereof.

Rule 9013. Motions: Form and Service

A request for an order, except when an application is authorized by these rules, shall be by written motion, unless made during a hearing. The motion shall state with particularity the grounds therefor, and shall set forth the relief or order sought. Every written motion other than one which may be considered ex parte, shall be served by the moving party within the time determined under Rule 9006(d). The moving party shall serve the motion on:

(a) the trustee or debtor in possession and on those entities specified by these rules; or

(b) the entities the court directs if these rules do not require service or specify the entities to be served.

Rule 9014. Contested Matters

(a) **Motion**. In a contested matter not otherwise governed by these rules, relief shall be requested by motion, and reasonable notice and opportunity for hearing shall be afforded the party against whom relief is sought. No response is required under this rule unless the court directs otherwise.

(b) **Service**. The motion shall be served in the manner provided for service of a summons and complaint by Rule 7004 and within the time determined under Rule 9006(d). Any written response to the motion shall be served within the time determined under Rule 9006(d). Any paper served after the motion shall be served in the manner provided by Rule 5(b) F. R. Civ. P.

(c) **Application of Part VII Rules**. Except as otherwise provided in this rule, and unless the court directs otherwise, the following rules shall apply: 7009, 7017, 7021, 7025, 7026, 7028-7037, 7041, 7042, 7052, 7054-7056, 7064, 7069, and 7071. The following subdivisions of Fed. R. Civ. P. 26, as incorporated by Rule 7026, shall not apply in a contested matter unless the court directs otherwise: 26(a)(1) (mandatory disclosure), 26(a)(2) (disclosures regarding expert testimony) and 26(a)(3) (additional pre-trial disclosure), and 26(f) (mandatory meeting before scheduling conference/discovery plan). An entity that desires to perpetuate testimony may proceed in the same manner as provided in Rule 7027 for the taking of a deposition before an adversary proceeding. The court may at any stage in a particular matter direct that one or more of the other rules in Part VII shall apply. The court shall give the parties notice of any order issued under this paragraph to afford them a reasonable opportunity to comply with the procedures prescribed by the order.

(d) **Testimony of Witnesses**. Testimony of witnesses with respect to disputed material factual issues shall be taken in the same manner as testimony in an adversary proceeding.

(e) **Attendance of Witnesses**. The court shall provide procedures that enable parties to ascertain at a reasonable time before any scheduled hearing whether the hearing will be an evidentiary hearing at which witnesses may testify.

Rule 9015. Jury Trials

(a) **Applicability of Certain Federal Rules of Civil Procedure**. Rules 38,39,47-49, and51, F. R. Civ. P., and Rule 81(c) F. R. Civ. P. insofar as it applies to jury trials, apply in cases and proceedings, except that a demand made under Rule 38(b) F. R. Civ. P. shall be filed in accordance with Rule 5005.

(b) **Consent to Have Trial Conducted by Bankruptcy Judge**. If the right to a jury trial applies, a timely demand has been filed pursuant to Rule 38(b) F. R. Civ. P., and the bankruptcy judge has been specially designated to conduct the jury trial, the parties may consent to have a jury trial conducted by a bankruptcy judge under 28 U.S.C. § 157(e)by jointly or separately filing a statement of consent within any applicable time limits specified by local rule.

(c) **Applicability of Rule 50 F. R. Civ. P**. Rule 50 F. R. Civ. P. applies in cases and proceedings, except that any renewed motion for judgment or request for a new trial shall be filed no later than 14 days after the entry of judgment.

Rule 9016. Subpoena

Rule 45 F. R. Civ. P. applies in cases under the Code.

Rule 9017. Evidence

The Federal Rules of Evidence and Rules 43, 44 and 44.1 F. R. Civ. P. apply in cases under the Code.

Rule 9018. Secret, Confidential, Scandalous, or Defamatory Matter

On motion or on its own initiative, with or without notice, the court may make any order which justice requires (1) to protect the estate or any entity in respect of a trade secret or other confidential research, development, or commercial information, (2) to protect any entity against scandalous or defamatory matter contained in any paper filed in a case under the Code, or (3) to protect governmental matters that are made confidential by statute or regulation. If an order is entered under this rule without notice, any entity affected thereby may move to vacate or modify the order, and after a hearing on notice the court shall determine the motion.

Rule 9019. Compromise and Arbitration

(a) Compromise. On motion by the trustee and after notice and a hearing, the court may approve a compromise or settlement. Notice shall be given to creditors, the United States trustee, the debtor, and indenture trustees as provided in Rule 2002 and to any other entity as the court may direct.
(b) Authority to Compromise or Settle Controversies Within Classes. After a hearing on such notice as the court may direct, the court may fix a class or classes of controversies and authorize the trustee to compromise or settle controversies within such class or classes without further hearing or notice.
(c) Arbitration. On stipulation of the parties to any controversy affecting the estate the court may authorize the matter to be submitted to final and binding arbitration.

Rule 9020. Contempt Proceedings

Rule 9014 governs a motion for an order of contempt made by the United States trustee or a party in interest.

Rule 9021. Entry of Judgment

A judgment or order is effective when entered under Rule 5003.

Rule 9022. Notice of Judgment or Order

(a) **Judgment or Order of Bankruptcy Judge**. Immediately on the entry of a judgment or order the clerk shall serve a notice of entry in the manner provided in Rule 5(b) F. R. Civ. P. on the contesting parties and on other entities as the court directs. Unless the case is a chapter 9 municipality case, the clerk shall forthwith transmit to the United States trustee a copy of the judgment or order. Service of the notice shall be noted in the docket. Lack of notice of the entry does not affect the time to appeal or relieve or authorize the court to relieve a party for failure to appeal within the time allowed, except as permitted in Rule 8002.
(b) **Judgment or Order of District Judge**. Notice of a judgment or order entered by a district judge is governed by Rule 77(d) F. R. Civ. P. Unless the case is a chapter 9 municipality case, the clerk shall forthwith transmit to the United States trustee a copy of a judgment or order entered by a district judge.

Rule 9023. New Trials; Amendment of Judgments

Except as provided in this rule and Rule 3008, Rule 59 F. R. Civ. P. applies in cases under the Code. A motion for a new trial or to alter or amend a judgment shall be filed, and a court may on its own order a new trial, no later than 14 days after entry of judgment. In some circumstances, Rule 8008 governs post-judgment motion practice after an appeal has been docketed and is pending.

Rule 9024. Relief from Judgment or Order

Rule 60 F. R. Civ. P. applies in cases under the Code except that (1) a motion to reopen a case under the Code or for the reconsideration of an order allowing or disallowing a claim against the estate entered without a contest is not subject to the one year limitation prescribed in Rule 60(c), (2) a complaint to revoke a discharge in a chapter 7 liquidation case may be filed only within the time allowed by § 727(e) of the Code, and (3) a complaint to revoke an order confirming a plan may be filed only within the time allowed by § 1144, § 1230, or § 1330. In some circumstances, Rule 8008 governs post-judgment motion practice after an appeal has been docketed and is pending.

Rule 9025. Security: Proceedings Against Sureties

Whenever the Code or these rules require or permit the giving of security by a party, and security is given in the form of a bond or stipulation or other undertaking with one or more sureties, each surety submits to the jurisdiction of the court, and liability may be determined in an adversary proceeding governed by the rules in Part VII.

Rule 9026. Exceptions Unnecessary

Rule 46 F. R. Civ. P. applies in cases under the Code.

Rule 9027. Removal

(a) **Notice of Removal.**
  (1) *Where Filed; Form and Content.* A notice of removal shall be filed with the clerk for the district and division within which is located the state or federal court where the civil action is pending. The notice shall be signed pursuant to Rule 9011 and contain a short and plain statement of the facts which entitle the party filing the notice to remove, contain a statement that upon removal of the claim or cause of action the party filing the notice does or does not consent to entry of final orders or judgment by the bankruptcy court, and be accompanied by a copy of all process and pleadings.
  (2) *Time for Filing; Civil Action Initiated Before Commencement of the Case Under the Code.* If the claim or cause of action in a civil action is pending when a case under the Code is commenced, a notice of removal may be filed only within the longest of (A) 90 days after the order for relief in the case under the Code, (B) 30 days after entry of

an order terminating a stay, if the claim or cause of action in a civil action has been stayed under § 362 of the Code, or (C) 30 days after a trustee qualifies in a chapter 11 reorganization case but not later than 180 days after the order for relief.

(3) *Time for Filing; Civil Action Initiated After Commencement of the Case Under the Code.* If a claim or cause of action is asserted in another court after the commencement of a case under the Code, a notice of removal may be filed with the clerk only within the shorter of (A) 30 days after receipt, through service or otherwise, of a copy of the initial pleading setting forth the claim or cause of action sought to be removed, or (B) 30 days after receipt of the summons if the initial pleading has been filed with the court but not served with the summons.

(b) **Notice.** Promptly after filing the notice of removal, the party filing the notice shall serve a copy of it on all parties to the removed claim or cause of action.

(c) **Filing in Non-Bankruptcy Court.** Promptly after filing the notice of removal, the party filing the notice shall file a copy of it with the clerk of the court from which the claim or cause of action is removed. Removal of the claim or cause of action is effected on such filing of a copy of the notice of removal. The parties shall proceed no further in that court unless and until the claim or cause of action is remanded.

(d) **Remand.** A motion for remand of the removed claim or cause of action shall be governed by Rule 9014 and served on the parties to the removed claim or cause of action.

(e) **Procedure After Removal.**

(1) After removal of a claim or cause of action to a district court the district court or, if the case under the Code has been referred to a bankruptcy judge of the district, the bankruptcy judge, may issue all necessary orders and process to bring before it all proper parties whether served by process issued by the court from which the claim or cause of action was removed or otherwise.

(2) The district court or, if the case under the Code has been referred to a bankruptcy judge of the district, the bankruptcy judge, may require the party filing the notice of removal to file with the clerk copies of all records and proceedings relating to the claim or cause of action in the court from which the claim or cause of action was removed.

(3) Any party who has filed a pleading in connection with the removed claim or cause of action, other than the party filing the notice of removal, shall file a statement that the party does or does not consent to entry of final orders or judgment by the bankruptcy court. A statement required by this paragraph shall be signed pursuant to Rule 9011 and shall be filed not later than 14 days after the filing of the notice of removal. Any party who files a statement pursuant to this paragraph shall mail a copy to every other party to the removed claim or cause of action.

(f) **Process After Removal**. If one or more of the defendants has not been served with process, the service has not been perfected prior to removal, or the process served proves to be defective, such process or service may be completed or new process issued pursuant to Part VII of these rules. This subdivision shall not deprive any defendant on whom process is served after removal of the defendant's right to move to remand the case.

(g) **Applicability of Part VII**. The rules of Part VII apply to a claim or cause of action removed to a district court from a federal or state court and govern procedure after removal. Repleading is not necessary unless the court so orders. In a removed action in which the defendant has not answered, the defendant shall answer or present the other defenses or objections available under the rules of Part VII within 21 days following the receipt through service or otherwise of a copy of the initial pleading setting forth the claim for relief on which the action or proceeding is based, or within 21 days following the service of summons on such initial pleading, or within seven days following the filing of the notice of removal, whichever period is longest.

(h) **Record Supplied**. When a party is entitled to copies of the records and proceedings in any civil action or proceeding in a federal or a state court, to be used in the removed civil action or proceeding, and the clerk of the federal or state court, on demand accompanied by payment or tender of the lawful fees, fails to deliver certified copies, the court may, on affidavit reciting the facts, direct such record to be supplied by affidavit or otherwise. Thereupon the proceedings, trial and judgment may be had in the court, and all process awarded, as if certified copies had been filed.

(i) **Attachment or Sequestration; Securities**. When a claim or cause of action is removed to a district court, any attachment or sequestration of property in the court from which the claim or cause of action was removed shall hold the property to answer the final judgment or decree in the same manner as the property would have been held to answer final judgment or decree had it been rendered by the court from which the claim or cause of action was removed. All bonds, undertakings, or security given by either party to the claim or cause of action prior to its removal shall remain valid and effectual notwithstanding such removal. All injunctions issued, orders entered and other proceedings had prior to removal shall remain in full force and effect until dissolved or modified by the court.

Rule 9028. Disability of a Judge

Rule 63 F. R. Civ. P. applies in cases under the Code.

Rule 9029. Local Bankruptcy Rules; Procedure When There is No Controlling Law

(a) **Local Bankruptcy Rules.**

(1) Each district court acting by a majority of its district judges may make and amend rules governing practice and procedure in all cases and proceedings within the district court's bankruptcy jurisdiction which are consistent with—but not duplicative of—Acts of Congress and these rules and which do not prohibit or limit the use of the Official Forms. Rule 83 F. R. Civ. P. governs the procedure for making local rules. A district court may authorize the bankruptcy judges of the district, subject to any limitation or condition it may prescribe and the requirements of 83 F. R. Civ. P., to make and amend rules of practice and procedure which are consistent with—but not duplicative of—Acts of Congress and these rules and which do not prohibit or limit the use of the Official Forms. Local rules shall conform to any uniform numbering system prescribed by the Judicial Conference of the United States.

(2) A local rule imposing a requirement of form shall not be enforced in a manner that causes a party to lose rights because of a nonwillful failure to comply with the requirement.

(b) **Procedure When There is No Controlling Law**. A judge may regulate practice in any manner consistent with federal law, these rules, Official Forms, and local rules of the district. No sanction or other disadvantage may be imposed for noncompliance with any requirement not in federal law, federal rules, Official Forms, or the local rules of the district unless the alleged violator has been furnished in the particular case with actual notice of the requirement.

Rule 9030. Jurisdiction and Venue Unaffected

These rules shall not be construed to extend or limit the jurisdiction of the courts or the venue of any matters therein.

Rule 9031. Masters Not Authorized

Rule 53 F. R. Civ. P. does not apply in cases under the Code.

Rule 9032. Effect of Amendment of Federal Rules of Civil Procedure

The Federal Rules of Civil Procedure which are incorporated by reference and made applicable by these rules shall be the Federal Rules of Civil Procedure in effect on the effective date of these rules and as thereafter amended, unless otherwise provided by such amendment or by these rules.

Rule 9033. Proposed Findings of Fact and Conclusions of Law

(a) **Service**. In a proceeding in which the bankruptcy court has issued proposed findings of fact and conclusions of law, the clerk shall serve forthwith copies on all parties by mail and note the date of mailing on the docket.

(b) **Objections: Time for Filing**. Within 14 days after being served with a copy of the proposed findings of fact and conclusions of law a party may serve and file with the clerk written objections which identify the specific proposed findings or conclusions objected to and state the grounds for such objection. A party may respond to another party's objections within 14 days after being served with a copy thereof. A party objecting to the bankruptcy judge's proposed findings or conclusions shall arrange promptly for the transcription of the record, or such portions of it as all parties may agree upon or the bankruptcy judge deems sufficient, unless the district judge otherwise directs.

(c) **Extension of Time**. The bankruptcy judge may for cause extend the time for filing objections by any party for a period not to exceed 21 days from the expiration of the time otherwise prescribed by this rule. A request to extend the time for filing objections must be made before the time for filing objections has expired, except that a request made no more than 21 days after the expiration of the time for filing objections may be granted upon a showing of excusable neglect.

(d) **Standard of Review**. The district judge shall make a de novo review upon the record or, after additional evidence, of any portion of the bankruptcy judge's findings of fact or conclusions of law to which specific written objection has been made in accordance with this rule. The district judge may accept, reject, or modify the proposed findings of fact or conclusions of law, receive further evidence, or recommit the matter to the bankruptcy judge with instructions.

Rule 9034. Transmittal of Pleadings, Motion Papers, Objections, and Other Papers to the United States Trustee

Unless the United States trustee requests otherwise or the case is a chapter 9 municipality case, any entity that files a pleading, motion, objection, or similar paper relating to any of the following matters shall transmit a copy thereof to the United States trustee within the time required by these rules for service of the paper:

(a) a proposed use, sale, or lease of property of the estate other than in the ordinary course of business;

(b) the approval of a compromise or settlement of a controversy;

(c) the dismissal or conversion of a case to another chapter;

(d) the employment of professional persons;

(e) an application for compensation or reimbursement of expenses;

(f) a motion for, or approval of an agreement relating to, the use of cash collateral or authority to obtain credit;

(g) the appointment of a trustee or examiner in a chapter 11 reorganization case; (h) the approval of a disclosure statement;

(h) the confirmation of a plan;

(i) an objection to, or waiver or revocation of, the debtor's discharge;

(j) any other matter in which the United States trustee requests copies of filed papers or the court orders copies transmitted to the United States trustee.

Rule 9035. Applicability of Rules in Judicial Districts in Alabama and North Carolina

In any case under the Code that is filed in or transferred to a district in the State of Alabama or the State of North Carolina and in which a United States trustee is not authorized to act, these rules apply to the extent that they are not inconsistent with any federal statute effective in the case.

Rule 9036. Notice by Electronic Transmission

Whenever the clerk or some other person as directed by the court is required to send notice by mail and the entity entitled to receive the notice requests in writing that, instead of notice by mail, all or part of the information required to be contained in the notice be sent by a specified type of electronic transmission, the court may direct the clerk or other person to send the information by such electronic transmission. Notice by electronic means is complete on transmission.

Rule 9037. Privacy Protection for Filings Made with the Court

(a) **Redacted Filings.** Unless the court orders otherwise, in an electronic or paper filing made with the court that contains an individual's social-security number, taxpayer-identification number, or birth date, the name of an individual, other than the debtor, known to be and identified as a minor, or a financial-account number, a party or nonparty making the filing may include only:
    (1) the last four digits of the social-security number and taxpayer-identification number;
    (2) the year of the individual's birth;
    (3) the minor's initials; and
    (4) the last four digits of the financial-account number.
(b) **Exemptions from the Redaction Requirement.** The redaction requirement does not apply to the following:
    (1) a financial-account number that identifies the property allegedly subject to forfeiture in a forfeiture proceeding;
    (2) the record of an administrative or agency proceeding unless filed with a proof of claim;
    (3) the official record of a state-court proceeding;
    (4) the record of a court or tribunal, if that record was not subject to the redaction requirement when originally filed;
    (5) a filing covered by subdivision (c) of this rule; and
    (6) a filing that is subject to § 110 of the Code.
(c) **Filings Made Under Seal.** The court may order that a filing be made under seal without redaction. The court may later unseal the filing or order the entity that made the filing to file a redacted version for the public record.

(d) **Protective Orders**. For cause, the court may by order in a case under the Code:

    (1) require redaction of additional information; or

    (2) limit or prohibit a nonparty's remote electronic access to a document filed with the court.

(e) **Option for Additional Unredacted Filing Under Seal**. An entity making a redacted filing may also file an unredacted copy under seal. The court must retain the unredacted copy as part of the record.

(f) **Option for Filing a Reference List**. A filing that contains redacted information may be filed together with a reference list that identifies each item of redacted information and specifies an appropriate identifier that uniquely corresponds to each item listed. The list must be filed under seal and may be amended as of right. Any reference in the case to a listed identifier will be construed to refer to the corresponding item of information.

(g) **Waiver of Protection of Identifiers**. An entity waives the protection of subdivision (a) as to the entity's own information by filing it without redaction and not under seal.

United States Code
Title 28 Provisions Relating to Bankruptcy

Title 28 – Judiciary and Judicial Procedure

Chapter 6 – Bankruptcy Judges

§151 - Designation of bankruptcy courts

In each judicial district, the bankruptcy judges in regular active service shall constitute a unit of the district court to be known as the bankruptcy court for that district. Each bankruptcy judge, as a judicial officer of the district court, may exercise the authority conferred under this chapter with respect to any action, suit, or proceeding and may preside alone and hold a regular or special session of the court, except as otherwise provided by law or by rule or order of the district court.

§152 - Appointment of bankruptcy judges

(a)

    (1) Each bankruptcy judge to be appointed for a judicial district, as provided in paragraph (2), shall be appointed by the court of appeals of the United States for the circuit in which such district is located. Such appointments shall be made after considering the recommendations of the Judicial Conference submitted pursuant to subsection (b). Each bankruptcy judge shall be appointed for a term of fourteen years, subject to the provisions of subsection (e). However, upon the expiration of the term, a bankruptcy judge may, with the approval of the judicial council of the circuit, continue to perform the duties of the office until the earlier of the date which is 180 days after the expiration of the term or the date of the appointment of a successor. Bankruptcy judges shall serve as judicial officers of the United States district court established under Article III of the Constitution.

    (2) The bankruptcy judges appointed pursuant to this section shall be appointed for the several judicial districts as follows:

Districts	Judges
Alabama:	
Northern	5
Middle	2
Southern	2
Alaska	2
Arizona	7
Arkansas:	
Eastern and Western	3

Districts	**Judges**
California:	
Northern	9
Eastern	6
Central	21
Southern	4
Colorado	5
Connecticut	3
Delaware	1
District of Columbia	1
Florida:	
Northern	1
Middle	8
Southern	5
Georgia:	
Northern	8
Middle	3
Southern	2
Hawaii	1
Idaho	2
Illinois:	
Northern	10
Central	3
Southern	1
Indiana:	
Northern	3
Southern	4
Iowa:	
Northern	2
Southern	2
Kansas	4
Kentucky:	
Eastern	2
Western	3
Louisiana:	
Eastern	2

Districts	Judges
Middle	1
Western	3
Maine	2
Maryland	4
Massachusetts	5
Michigan:	
Eastern	4
Western	3
Minnesota	4
Mississippi:	
Northern	1
Southern	2
Missouri:	
Eastern	3
Western	3
Montana	1
Nebraska	2
Nevada	3
New Hampshire	1
New Jersey	8
New Mexico	2
New York:	
Northern	2
Southern	9
Eastern	6
Western	3
North Carolina:	
Eastern	2
Middle	2
Western	2
North Dakota	1
Ohio:	
Northern	8
Southern	7
Oklahoma:	

Districts	**Judges**
Northern	2
Eastern	1
Western	3
Oregon	5
Pennsylvania:	
Eastern	5
Middle	2
Western	4
Puerto Rico	2
Rhode Island	1
South Carolina	2
South Dakota	2
Tennessee:	
Eastern	3
Middle	3
Western	4
Texas:	
Northern	6
Eastern	2
Southern	6
Western	4
Utah	3
Vermont	1
Virginia:	
Eastern	5
Western	3
Washington:	
Eastern	2
Western	5
West Virginia:	
Northern	1
Southern	1
Wisconsin:	
Eastern	4
Western	2

Districts	**Judges**
Wyoming	1.

(1) Whenever a majority of the judges of any court of appeals cannot agree upon the appointment of a bankruptcy judge, the chief judge of such court shall make such appointment.

(2) The judges of the district courts for the territories shall serve as the bankruptcy judges for such courts. The United States court of appeals for the circuit within which such a territorial district court is located may appoint bankruptcy judges under this chapter for such district if authorized to do so by the Congress of the United States under this section.

(b)

(1) The Judicial Conference of the United States shall, from time to time, and after considering the recommendations submitted by the Director of the Administrative Office of the United States Courts after such Director has consulted with the judicial council of the circuit involved, determine the official duty stations of bankruptcy judges and places of holding court.

(2) The Judicial Conference shall, from time to time, submit recommendations to the Congress regarding the number of bankruptcy judges needed and the districts in which such judges are needed.

(3) Not later than December 31, 1994, and not later than the end of each 2-year period thereafter, the Judicial Conference of the United States shall conduct a comprehensive review of all judicial districts to assess the continuing need for the bankruptcy judges authorized by this section, and shall report to the Congress its findings and any recommendations for the elimination of any authorized position which can be eliminated when a vacancy exists by reason of resignation, retirement, removal, or death.

(c)

(1) Each bankruptcy judge may hold court at such places within the judicial district, in addition to the official duty station of such judge, as the business of the court may require.

(2)

(A) Bankruptcy judges may hold court at such places within the United States outside the judicial district as the nature of the business of the court may require, and upon such notice as the court orders, upon a finding by either the chief judge of the bankruptcy court (or, if the chief judge is unavailable, the most senior available bankruptcy judge) or by the judicial council of the circuit that, because of emergency conditions, no location within the district is reasonably available where the bankruptcy judges could hold court.

(B) Bankruptcy judges may transact any business at special sessions of court held outside the district pursuant to this paragraph that might be transacted at a regular session.

(C) If a bankruptcy court issues an order exercising its authority under subparagraph (A), the court—

    (i) through the Administrative Office of the United States Courts, shall—

        (I) send notice of such order, including the reasons for the issuance of such order, to the Committee on the Judiciary of the Senate and the Committee on the Judiciary of the House of Representatives; and

        (II) not later than 180 days after the expiration of such court order submit a brief report to the Committee on the Judiciary of the Senate and the Committee on the Judiciary of the House of Representatives describing the impact of such order, including—

          (aa) the reasons for the issuance of such order;

          (bb) the duration of such order;

          (cc) the impact of such order on litigants; and

          (dd) the costs to the judiciary resulting from such order; and

    (ii) shall provide reasonable notice to the United States Marshals Service before the commencement of any special session held pursuant to such order.

(d) With the approval of the Judicial Conference and of each of the judicial councils involved, a bankruptcy judge may be designated to serve in any district adjacent to or near the district for which such bankruptcy judge was appointed.

(e) A bankruptcy judge may be removed during the term for which such bankruptcy judge is appointed, only for incompetence, misconduct, neglect of duty, or physical or mental disability and only by the judicial council of the circuit in which the judge's official duty station is located. Removal may not occur unless a majority of all of the judges of such council concur in the order of removal. Before any order of removal may be entered, a full specification of charges shall be furnished to such bankruptcy judge who shall be accorded an opportunity to be heard on such charges.

§153 - Salaries; character of service

(a) Each bankruptcy judge shall serve on a full-time basis and shall receive as full compensation for his services, a salary at an annual rate that is equal to

92 percent of the salary of a judge of the district court of the United States as determined pursuant to section 135, to be paid at such times as the Judicial Conference of the United States determines.

(b) A bankruptcy judge may not engage in the practice of law and may not engage in any other practice, business, occupation, or employment inconsistent with the expeditious, proper, and impartial performance of such bankruptcy judge's duties as a judicial officer. The Conference may promulgate appropriate rules and regulations to implement this subsection.

(c) Each individual appointed under this chapter shall take the oath or affirmation prescribed by section 453 of this title before performing the duties of the office of bankruptcy judge.

(d) A bankruptcy judge appointed under this chapter shall be exempt from the provisions of subchapter I of chapter 63 of title 5.

§154 - Division of businesses; chief judge

(a) Each bankruptcy court for a district having more than one bankruptcy judge shall by majority vote promulgate rules for the division of business among the bankruptcy judges to the extent that the division of business is not otherwise provided for by the rules of the district court.

(b) In each district court having more than one bankruptcy judge the district court shall designate one judge to serve as chief judge of such bankruptcy court. Whenever a majority of the judges of such district court cannot agree upon the designation as chief judge, the chief judge of such district court shall make such designation. The chief judge of the bankruptcy court shall ensure that the rules of the bankruptcy court and of the district court are observed and that the business of the bankruptcy court is handled effectively and expeditiously.

§155 - Temporary transfer of bankruptcy judges

(a) A bankruptcy judge may be transferred to serve temporarily as a bankruptcy judge in any judicial district other than the judicial district for which such bankruptcy judge was appointed upon the approval of the judicial council of each of the circuits involved.

(b) A bankruptcy judge who has retired may, upon consent, be recalled to serve as a bankruptcy judge in any judicial district by the judicial council of the circuit within which such district is located. Upon recall, a bankruptcy judge may receive a salary for such service in accordance with regulations promulgated by the Judicial Conference of the United States, subject to the restrictions on the payment of an annuity in section 377 of this title or in subchapter III of chapter 83, and chapter 84, of title 5 which are applicable to such judge.

§156 - Staff; expenses

(a) Each bankruptcy judge may appoint a secretary, a law clerk, and such additional assistants as the Director of the Administrative Office of the United States Courts determines to be necessary. A law clerk appointed under this section shall be exempt from the provisions of subchapter I of chapter 63 of title 5, unless specifically included by the appointing judge or by local rule of court.

(b) Upon certification to the judicial council of the circuit involved and to the Director of the Administrative Office of the United States Courts that the number of cases and proceedings pending within the jurisdiction under section 1334 of this title within a judicial district so warrants, the bankruptcy judges for such district may appoint an individual to serve as clerk of such bankruptcy court. The clerk may appoint, with the approval of such bankruptcy judges, and in such number as may be approved by the Director, necessary deputies, and may remove such deputies with the approval of such bankruptcy judges.

(c) Any court may utilize facilities or services, either on or off the court's premises, which pertain to the provision of notices, dockets, calendars, and other administrative information to parties in cases filed under the provisions of title 11, United States Code, where the costs of such facilities or services are paid for out of the assets of the estate and are not charged to the United States. The utilization of such facilities or services shall be subject to such conditions and limitations as the pertinent circuit council may prescribe.

(d) No office of the bankruptcy clerk of court may be consolidated with the district clerk of court office without the prior approval of the Judicial Conference and the Congress.

(e) In a judicial district where a bankruptcy clerk has been appointed pursuant to subsection (b), the bankruptcy clerk shall be the official custodian of the records and dockets of the bankruptcy court.

(f) For purposes of financial accountability in a district where a bankruptcy clerk has been certified, such clerk shall be accountable for and pay into the Treasury all fees, costs, and other monies collected by such clerk except uncollected fees not required by an Act of Congress to be prepaid. Such clerk shall make returns thereof to the Director of the Administrative Office of the United States Courts and the Director of the Executive Office For United States Trustees, under regulations prescribed by such Directors.

§157 – Procedures

(a) Each district court may provide that any or all cases under title 11 and any or all proceedings arising under title 11 or arising in or related to a case under title 11 shall be referred to the bankruptcy judges for the district.

(b)

  (1) Bankruptcy judges may hear and determine all cases under title 11 and all core proceedings arising under title 11, or arising in a case under title 11, referred under subsection (a) of this section, and may enter appropriate orders and judgments, subject to review under section 158 of this title.

  (2) Core proceedings include, but are not limited to—

    (A) matters concerning the administration of the estate;

    (B) allowance or disallowance of claims against the estate or exemptions from property of the estate, and estimation of claims or interests for the purposes of confirming a plan under chapter 11, 12, or 13 of title 11but not the liquidation or estimation of contingent or unliquidated personal injury tort or wrongful death claims against the estate for purposes of distribution in a case under title 11;

    (C) counterclaims by the estate against persons filing claims against the estate;

    (D) orders in respect to obtaining credit;

    (E) orders to turn over property of the estate;

    (F) proceedings to determine, avoid, or recover preferences;

    (G) motions to terminate, annul, or modify the automatic stay;

    (H) proceedings to determine, avoid, or recover fraudulent conveyances;

    (I) determinations as to the dischargeability of particular debts;

    (J) objections to discharges;

    (K) determinations of the validity, extent, or priority of liens;

    (L) confirmations of plans;

    (M) orders approving the use or lease of property, including the use of cash collateral;

    (N) orders approving the sale of property other than property resulting from claims brought by the estate against persons who have not filed claims against the estate;

    (O) other proceedings affecting the liquidation of the assets of the estate or the adjustment of the debtor-creditor or the equity security holder relationship, except personal injury tort or wrongful death claims; and

    (P) recognition of foreign proceedings and other matters under chapter 15 of title 11.

  (3) The bankruptcy judge shall determine, on the judge's own motion or on timely motion of a party, whether a proceeding is a core proceeding under this subsection or is a proceeding that is otherwise related to a case under title 11. A determination that a proceeding is

not a core proceeding shall not be made solely on the basis that its resolution may be affected by State law.

(4) Non-core proceedings under section 157(b)(2)(B) of title 28, United States Code, shall not be subject to the mandatory abstention provisions of section 1334(c)(2).

(5) The district court shall order that personal injury tort and wrongful death claims shall be tried in the district court in which the bankruptcy case is pending, or in the district court in the district in which the claim arose, as determined by the district court in which the bankruptcy case is pending.

(c)

(1) A bankruptcy judge may hear a proceeding that is not a core proceeding but that is otherwise related to a case under title 11. In such proceeding, the bankruptcy judge shall submit proposed findings of fact and conclusions of law to the district court, and any final order or judgment shall be entered by the district judge after considering the bankruptcy judge's proposed findings and conclusions and after reviewing de novo those matters to which any party has timely and specifically objected.

(2) Notwithstanding the provisions of paragraph (1) of this subsection, the district court, with the consent of all the parties to the proceeding, may refer a proceeding related to a case under title 11 to a bankruptcy judge to hear and determine and to enter appropriate orders and judgments, subject to review under section 158 of this title.

(d) The district court may withdraw, in whole or in part, any case or proceeding referred under this section, on its own motion or on timely motion of any party, for cause shown. The district court shall, on timely motion of a party, so withdraw a proceeding if the court determines that resolution of the proceeding requires consideration of both title 11 and other laws of the United States regulating organizations or activities affecting interstate commerce.

(e) If the right to a jury trial applies in a proceeding that may be heard under this section by a bankruptcy judge, the bankruptcy judge may conduct the jury trial if specially designated to exercise such jurisdiction by the district court and with the express consent of all the parties.

§158 – Appeals

(a) The district courts of the United States shall have jurisdiction to hear appeals

(1) from final judgments, orders, and decrees;

(2) from interlocutory orders and decrees issued under section 1121(d) of title 11 increasing or reducing the time periods referred to in section 1121 of such title; and

(3) with leave of the court, from other interlocutory orders and decrees; and, with leave of the court, from interlocutory orders and decrees, of bankruptcy judges entered in cases and proceedings referred to the bankruptcy judges under section 157 of this title. An appeal under this subsection shall be taken only to the district court for the judicial district in which the bankruptcy judge is serving.

(b)

(1) The judicial council of a circuit shall establish a bankruptcy appellate panel service composed of bankruptcy judges of the districts in the circuit who are appointed by the judicial council in accordance with paragraph (3), to hear and determine, with the consent of all the parties, appeals under subsection (a) unless the judicial council finds that—

(A) there are insufficient judicial resources available in the circuit; or

(B) establishment of such service would result in undue delay or increased cost to parties in cases under title 11.

Not later than 90 days after making the finding, the judicial council shall submit to the Judicial Conference of the United States a report containing the factual basis of such finding.

(2)

(A) A judicial council may reconsider, at any time, the finding described in paragraph (1).

(B) On the request of a majority of the district judges in a circuit for which a bankruptcy appellate panel service is established under paragraph (1), made after the expiration of the 1-year period beginning on the date such service is established, the judicial council of the circuit shall determine whether a circumstance specified in subparagraph (A) or (B) of such paragraph exists.

(C) On its own motion, after the expiration of the 3-year period beginning on the date a bankruptcy appellate panel service is established under paragraph (1), the judicial council of the circuit may determine whether a circumstance specified in subparagraph (A) or (B) of such paragraph exists.

(D) If the judicial council finds that either of such circumstances exists, the judicial council may provide for the completion of the appeals then pending before such service and the orderly termination of such service.

(3) Bankruptcy judges appointed under paragraph (1) shall be appointed and may be reappointed under such paragraph.

(4) If authorized by the Judicial Conference of the United States, the judicial councils of 2 or more circuits may establish a joint bankruptcy appellate panel comprised of bankruptcy judges from the districts within the circuits for which such panel is established, to hear and determine, upon the consent of all the parties, appeals under subsection (a) of this section.

(5) An appeal to be heard under this subsection shall be heard by a panel of 3 members of the bankruptcy appellate panel service, except that a member of such service may not hear an appeal originating in the district for which such member is appointed or designated under section 152 of this title.

(6) Appeals may not be heard under this subsection by a panel of the bankruptcy appellate panel service unless the district judges for the district in which the appeals occur, by majority vote, have authorized such service to hear and determine appeals originating in such district.

(c)

(1) Subject to subsections (b) and (d)(2), each appeal under subsection (a) shall be heard by a 3-judge panel of the bankruptcy appellate panel service established under subsection (b)(1) unless—

    (A) the appellant elects at the time of filing the appeal; or

    (B) any other party elects, not later than 30 days after service of notice of the appeal;

to have such appeal heard by the district court.

(2) An appeal under subsections (a) and (b) of this section shall be taken in the same manner as appeals in civil proceedings generally are taken to the courts of appeals from the district courts and in the time provided by Rule 8002 of the Bankruptcy Rules.

(d)

(1) The courts of appeals shall have jurisdiction of appeals from all final decisions, judgments, orders, and decrees entered under subsections (a) and (b) of this section.

(2)

    (A) The appropriate court of appeals shall have jurisdiction of appeals described in the first sentence of subsection (a) if the bankruptcy court, the district court, or the bankruptcy appellate panel involved, acting on its own motion or on the request of a party to the judgment, order, or decree described in such first sentence, or all the appellants and appellees (if any) acting jointly, certify that—

        (i) the judgment, order, or decree involves a question of law as to which there is no controlling decision of the court of appeals for the circuit or of the Supreme Court of the United States, or involves a matter of public importance;

(ii) the judgment, order, or decree involves a question of law requiring resolution of conflicting decisions; or

(iii) an immediate appeal from the judgment, order, or decree may materially advance the progress of the case or proceeding in which the appeal is taken;

and if the court of appeals authorizes the direct appeal of the judgment, order, or decree.

(B) If the bankruptcy court, the district court, or the bankruptcy appellate panel—

(i) on its own motion or on the request of a party, determines that a circumstance specified in clause (i), (ii), or (iii) of subparagraph (A) exists; or

(ii) receives a request made by a majority of the appellants and a majority of appellees (if any) to make the certification described in subparagraph (A);

then the bankruptcy court, the district court, or the bankruptcy appellate panel shall make the certification described in subparagraph (A).

(C) The parties may supplement the certification with a short statement of the basis for the certification.

(D) An appeal under this paragraph does not stay any proceeding of the bankruptcy court, the district court, or the bankruptcy appellate panel from which the appeal is taken, unless the respective bankruptcy court, district court, or bankruptcy appellate panel, or the court of appeals in which the appeal is pending, issues a stay of such proceeding pending the appeal.

(E) Any request under subparagraph (B) for certification shall be made not later than 60 days after the entry of the judgment, order, or decree.

§159 - Bankruptcy statistics

(a) The clerk of the district court, or the clerk of the bankruptcy court if one is certified pursuant to section 156(b) of this title, shall collect statistics regarding debtors who are individuals with primarily consumer debts seeking relief under chapters 7, 11, and 13 of title 11. Those statistics shall be in a standardized format prescribed by the Director of the Administrative Office of the United States Courts (referred to in this section as the "Director").

(b) The Director shall—

(1) compile the statistics referred to in subsection (a);

(2) make the statistics available to the public; and

(3) not later than July 1, 2008, and annually thereafter, prepare, and submit to Congress a report concerning the information collected under subsection (a) that contains an analysis of the information.

(c) The compilation required under subsection (b) shall—

   (1) be itemized, by chapter, with respect to title 11;

   (2) be presented in the aggregate and for each district; and

   (3) include information concerning—

      (A) the total assets and total liabilities of the debtors described in subsection (a), and in each category of assets and liabilities, as reported in the schedules prescribed pursuant to section 2075 of this title and filed by debtors;

      (B) the current monthly income, average income, and average expenses of debtors as reported on the schedules and statements that each such debtor files under sections 521 and 1322 of title 11;

      (C) the aggregate amount of debt discharged in cases filed during the reporting period, determined as the difference between the total amount of debt and obligations of a debtor reported on the schedules and the amount of such debt reported in categories which are predominantly nondischargeable;

      (D) the average period of time between the date of the filing of the petition and the closing of the case for cases closed during the reporting period;

      (E) for cases closed during the reporting period—

         (i) the number of cases in which a reaffirmation agreement was filed; and

         (ii)

            (I) the total number of reaffirmation agreements filed;

            (II) of those cases in which a reaffirmation agreement was filed, the number of cases in which the debtor was not represented by an attorney; and

            (III) of those cases in which a reaffirmation agreement was filed, the number of cases in which the reaffirmation agreement was approved by the court;

      (F) with respect to cases filed under chapter 13 of title 11, for the reporting period—

         (i)

            (I) the number of cases in which a final order was entered determining the value of property securing a claim in an amount less than the amount of the claim; and

            (II) the number of final orders entered determining the value of property securing a claim;

      (ii) the number of cases dismissed, the number of cases dismissed for failure to make payments under the plan, the number of cases refiled after dismissal, and the number of cases in which the plan was completed, separately itemized with respect to the number of modifications made before completion of the plan, if any; and

      (iii) the number of cases in which the debtor filed another case during the 6-year period preceding the filing;

    (G) the number of cases in which creditors were fined for misconduct and any amount of punitive damages awarded by the court for creditor misconduct; and

    (H) the number of cases in which sanctions under rule 9011 of the Federal Rules of Bankruptcy Procedure were imposed against the debtor's attorney or damages awarded under such Rule.

Chapter 39 – United States Trustees

§581 - United States trustees

(a) The Attorney General shall appoint one United States trustee for each of the following regions composed of Federal judicial districts (without regard to section 451):

(1) The judicial districts established for the States of Maine, Massachusetts, New Hampshire, and Rhode Island.

(2) The judicial districts established for the States of Connecticut, New York, and Vermont.

(3) The judicial districts established for the States of Delaware, New Jersey, and Pennsylvania.

(4) The judicial districts established for the States of Maryland, North Carolina, South Carolina, Virginia, and West Virginia and for the District of Columbia.

(5) The judicial districts established for the States of Louisiana and Mississippi.

(6) The Northern District of Texas and the Eastern District of Texas.

(7) The Southern District of Texas and the Western District of Texas.

(8) The judicial districts established for the States of Kentucky and Tennessee.

(9) The judicial districts established for the States of Michigan and Ohio.

(10) The Central District of Illinois and the Southern District of Illinois; and the judicial districts established for the State of Indiana.

(11) The Northern District of Illinois; and the judicial districts established for the State of Wisconsin.

(12) The judicial districts established for the States of Minnesota, Iowa, North Dakota, and South Dakota.

(13) The judicial districts established for the States of Arkansas, Nebraska, and Missouri.

(14) The District of Arizona.

(15) The Southern District of California; and the judicial districts established for the State of Hawaii, and for Guam and the Commonwealth of the Northern Mariana Islands.

(16) The Central District of California.

(17) The Eastern District of California and the Northern District of California; and the judicial district established for the State of Nevada.

(18) The judicial districts established for the States of Alaska, Idaho (exclusive of Yellowstone National Park), Montana (exclusive of Yellowstone National Park), Oregon, and Washington.

(19) The judicial districts established for the States of Colorado, Utah, and Wyoming (including those portions of Yellowstone National Park situated in the States of Montana and Idaho).

(20) The judicial districts established for the States of Kansas, New Mexico, and Oklahoma.

(21) The judicial districts established for the States of Alabama, Florida, and Georgia and for the Commonwealth of Puerto Rico and the Virgin Islands of the United States.

(b) Each United States trustee shall be appointed for a term of five years. On the expiration of his term, a United States trustee shall continue to perform the duties of his office until his successor is appointed and qualifies.

(c) Each United States trustee is subject to removal by the Attorney General.

§582 - Assistant United States trustees

(a) The Attorney General may appoint one or more assistant United States trustees in any region when the public interest so requires.

(b) Each assistant United States trustee is subject to removal by the Attorney General.

§583 - Oath of office

Each United States trustee and assistant United States trustee, before taking office, shall take an oath to execute faithfully his duties.

§584 - Official stations

The Attorney General may determine the official stations of the United States trustees and assistant United States trustees within the regions for which they were appointed.

§585 – Vacancies

(a) The Attorney General may appoint an acting United States trustee for a region in which the office of the United States trustee is vacant. The individual so appointed may serve until the date on which the vacancy is filled by appointment under section 581 of this title or by designation under subsection (b) of this section.

(b) The Attorney General may designate a United States trustee to serve in not more than two regions for such time as the public interest requires.

§586 - Duties; supervision by Attorney General

(a) Each United States trustee, within the region for which such United States trustee is appointed, shall—

(1) establish, maintain, and supervise a panel of private trustees that are eligible and available to serve as trustees in cases under chapter 7 of title 11;

(2) serve as and perform the duties of a trustee in a case under title 11 when required under title 11 to serve as trustee in such a case;

(3) supervise the administration of cases and trustees in cases under chapter 7, 11, 12, 13, or 15 of title 11by, whenever the United States trustee considers it to be appropriate—

   (A)

   (i) reviewing, in accordance with procedural guidelines adopted by the Executive Office of the United States Trustee (which guidelines shall be applied uniformly by the United States trustee except when circumstances warrant different treatment), applications filed for compensation and reimbursement under section 330 of title 11; and

   (ii) filing with the court comments with respect to such application and, if the United States Trustee considers it to be appropriate, objections to such application;

   (B) monitoring plans and disclosure statements filed in cases under chapter 11 of title 11 and filing with the court, in connection with hearings under sections 1125 and 1128 of such title, comments with respect to such plans and disclosure statements;

   (C) monitoring plans filed under chapters 12 and 13 of title 11and filing with the court, in connection with hearings under sections 1224, 1229, 1324, and 1329 of such title, comments with respect to such plans;

   (D) taking such action as the United States trustee deems to be appropriate to ensure that all reports, schedules, and fees required to be filed under title 11 and this title by the debtor are properly and timely filed;

(E) monitoring creditors' committees appointed under title 11;

(F) notifying the appropriate United States attorney of matters which relate to the occurrence of any action which may constitute a crime under the laws of the United States and, on the request of the United States attorney, assisting the United States attorney in carrying out prosecutions based on such action;

(G) monitoring the progress of cases under title 11 and taking such actions as the United States trustee deems to be appropriate to prevent undue delay in such progress;

(H) in small business cases (as defined in section 101 of title 11), performing the additional duties specified in title 11 pertaining to such cases; and

(I) monitoring applications filed under section 327 of title 11 and, whenever the United States trustee deems it to be appropriate, filing with the court comments with respect to the approval of such applications;

(4) deposit or invest under section 345 of title 11 money received as trustee in cases under title 11;

(5) perform the duties prescribed for the United States trustee under title 11 and this title, and such duties consistent with title 11 and this title as the Attorney General may prescribe;

(6) make such reports as the Attorney General directs, including the results of audits performed under section 603(a) of the Bankruptcy Abuse Prevention and Consumer Protection Act of 2005;

(7) in each of such small business cases—

(A) conduct an initial debtor interview as soon as practicable after the date of the order for relief but before the first meeting scheduled under section 341(a) of title 11, at which time the United States trustee shall—

(i) begin to investigate the debtor's viability;

(ii) inquire about the debtor's business plan;

(iii) explain the debtor's obligations to file monthly operating reports and other required reports;

(iv) attempt to develop an agreed scheduling order; and

(v) inform the debtor of other obligations;

(B) if determined to be appropriate and advisable, visit the appropriate business premises of the debtor, ascertain the state of the debtor's books and records, and verify that the debtor has filed its tax returns; and

(C) review and monitor diligently the debtor's activities, to determine as promptly as possible whether the debtor will be unable to confirm a plan; and

(8) in any case in which the United States trustee finds material grounds for any relief under section 1112 of title 11, apply promptly after making that finding to the court for relief.

(b) If the number of cases under chapter 12 or 13 of title 11commenced in a particular region so warrants, the United States trustee for such region may, subject to the approval of the Attorney General, appoint one or more individuals to serve as standing trustee, or designate one or more assistant United States trustees to serve in cases under such chapter. The United States trustee for such region shall supervise any such individual appointed as standing trustee in the performance of the duties of standing trustee.

(c) Each United States trustee shall be under the general supervision of the Attorney General, who shall provide general coordination and assistance to the United States trustees.

(d)

    (1) The Attorney General shall prescribe by rule qualifications for membership on the panels established by United States trustees under paragraph (a)(1) of this section, and qualifications for appointment under subsection (b) of this section to serve as standing trustee in cases under chapter 12 or 13 of title 11. The Attorney General may not require that an individual be an attorney in order to qualify for appointment under subsection (b) of this section to serve as standing trustee in cases under chapter 12 or 13 of title 11.

    (2) A trustee whose appointment under subsection (a)(1) or under subsection (b) is terminated or who ceases to be assigned to cases filed under title 11, United States Code, may obtain judicial review of the final agency decision by commencing an action in the district court of the United States for the district for which the panel to which the trustee is appointed under subsection (a)(1), or in the district court of the United States for the district in which the trustee is appointed under subsection (b) resides, after first exhausting all available administrative remedies, which if the trustee so elects, shall also include an administrative hearing on the record. Unless the trustee elects to have an administrative hearing on the record, the trustee shall be deemed to have exhausted all administrative remedies for purposes of this paragraph if the agency fails to make a final agency decision within 90 days after the trustee requests administrative remedies. The Attorney General shall prescribe procedures to implement this paragraph. The decision of the agency shall be affirmed by the district court unless it is unreasonable and without cause based on the administrative record before the agency.

(e)

    (1) The Attorney General, after consultation with a United States trustee that has appointed an individual under subsection (b) of this section to

serve as standing trustee in cases under chapter 12 or 13 of title 11, shall fix—

(A) a maximum annual compensation for such individual consisting of—

    (i) an amount not to exceed the highest annual rate of basic pay in effect for level V of the Executive Schedule; and

    (ii) the cash value of employment benefits comparable to the employment benefits provided by the United States to individuals who are employed by the United States at the same rate of basic pay to perform similar services during the same period of time; and

(B) a percentage fee not to exceed—

    (i) in the case of a debtor who is not a family farmer, ten percent; or

    (ii) in the case of a debtor who is a family farmer, the sum of—

        (I) not to exceed ten percent of the payments made under the plan of such debtor, with respect to payments in an aggregate amount not to exceed $450,000; and

        (II) three percent of payments made under the plan of such debtor, with respect to payments made after the aggregate amount of payments made under the plan exceeds $450,000;

    based on such maximum annual compensation and the actual, necessary expenses incurred by such individual as standing trustee.

(2) Such individual shall collect such percentage fee from all payments received by such individual under plans in the cases under chapter 12 or 13 of title 11 for which such individual serves as standing trustee. Such individual shall pay to the United States trustee, and the United States trustee shall deposit in the United States Trustee System Fund—

(A) any amount by which the actual compensation of such individual exceeds 5 per centum upon all payments received under plans in cases under chapter 12 or 13 of title 11 for which such individual serves as standing trustee; and

(B) any amount by which the percentage for all such cases exceeds—

    (i) such individual's actual compensation for such cases, as adjusted under subparagraph (A) of paragraph (1); plus

    (ii) the actual, necessary expenses incurred by such individual as standing trustee in such cases. Subject to the approval of the Attorney General, any or all of the interest earned from the deposit of payments under plans by such individual may be utilized to pay actual, necessary expenses without regard to the percentage limitation contained in subparagraph (d)(1)(B) of this section.

(3) After first exhausting all available administrative remedies, an individual appointed under subsection (b) may obtain judicial review of final agency action to deny a claim of actual, necessary expenses under this subsection by commencing an action in the district court of the United States for the district where the individual resides. The decision of the agency shall be affirmed by the district court unless it is unreasonable and without cause based upon the administrative record before the agency.

(4) The Attorney General shall prescribe procedures to implement this subsection.

(f)

(1) The United States trustee for each district is authorized to contract with auditors to perform audits in cases designated by the United States trustee, in accordance with the procedures established under section 603(a) of the Bankruptcy Abuse Prevention and Consumer Protection Act of 2005.

(2)

(A) The report of each audit referred to in paragraph (1) shall be filed with the court and transmitted to the United States trustee. Each report shall clearly and conspicuously specify any material misstatement of income or expenditures or of assets identified by the person performing the audit. In any case in which a material misstatement of income or expenditures or of assets has been reported, the clerk of the district court (or the clerk of the bankruptcy court if one is certified under section 156(b) of this title) shall give notice of the misstatement to the creditors in the case.

(B) If a material misstatement of income or expenditures or of assets is reported, the United States trustee shall—

(i) report the material misstatement, if appropriate, to the United States Attorney pursuant to section 3057 of title 18; and

(ii) if advisable, take appropriate action, including but not limited to commencing an adversary proceeding to revoke the debtor's discharge pursuant to section 727(d) of title 11.

§587 – Salaries

Subject to sections 5315 through 5317 of title 5, the Attorney General shall fix the annual salaries of United States trustees and assistant United States trustees at rates of compensation not in excess of the rate of basic compensation provided for Executive Level IV of the Executive Schedule set forth in section 5315 of title 5, United States Code.

§588 – Expenses

Necessary office expenses of the United States trustee shall be allowed when authorized by the Attorney General.

§589 - Staff and other employees

The United States trustee may employ staff and other employees on approval of the Attorney General.

§589a - United States Trustee System Fund

(a) There is hereby established in the Treasury of the United States a special fund to be known as the "United States Trustee System Fund" (hereinafter in this section referred to as the "Fund"). Monies in the Fund shall be available to the Attorney General without fiscal year limitation in such amounts as may be specified in appropriations Acts for the following purposes in connection with the operations of United States trustees—

    (1) salaries and related employee benefits;

    (2) travel and transportation;

    (3) rental of space;

    (4) communication, utilities, and miscellaneous computer charges;

    (5) security investigations and audits;

    (6) supplies, books, and other materials for legal research;

    (7) furniture and equipment;

    (8) miscellaneous services, including those obtained by contract; and

    (9) printing.

(b) For the purpose of recovering the cost of services of the United States Trustee System, there shall be deposited as offsetting collections to the appropriation "United States Trustee System Fund", to remain available until expended, the following—

    (1)

        (A) 40.46 percent of the fees collected under section 1930(a)(1)(A); and

        (B) 28.33 percent of the fees collected under section 1930(a)(1)(B);

    (2) 48.89 percent of the fees collected under section 1930(a)(3) of this title;

    (3) one-half of the fees collected under section 1930(a)(4) of this title;

    (4) one-half of the fees collected under section 1930(a)(5) of this title;

    (5) 100 percent of the fees collected under section 1930(a)(6) of this title;

    (6) three-fourths of the fees collected under the last sentence of section 1930(a) of this title;

    (7) the compensation of trustees received under section 330(d) of title 11 by the clerks of the bankruptcy courts;

    (8) excess fees collected under section 586(e)(2) of this title;

    (9) interest earned on Fund investment; and

    (10) fines imposed under section 110(l) of title 11, United States Code.

(c) Amounts in the Fund which are not currently needed for the purposes specified in subsection (a) shall be kept on deposit or invested in obligations of, or guaranteed by, the United States.

(d) The Attorney General shall transmit to the Congress, not later than 120 days after the end of each fiscal year, a detailed report on the amounts deposited in the Fund and a description of expenditures made under this section.

(e) There are authorized to be appropriated to the Fund for any fiscal year such sums as may be necessary to supplement amounts deposited under subsection (b) for the purposes specified in subsection (a).

§589b - Bankruptcy data

(a) Rules.—The Attorney General shall, within a reasonable time after the effective date of this section, issue rules requiring uniform forms for (and from time to time thereafter to appropriately modify and approve)—

    (1) final reports by trustees in cases under chapters 7, 12, and 13 of title 11; and

    (2) periodic reports by debtors in possession or trustees in cases under chapter 11 of title 11.

(b) Reports.—Each report referred to in subsection (a) shall be designed (and the requirements as to place and manner of filing shall be established) so as to facilitate compilation of data and maximum possible access of the public, both by physical inspection at one or more central filing locations, and by electronic access through the Internet or other appropriate media.

(c) Required Information.—The information required to be filed in the reports referred to in subsection (b) shall be that which is in the best interests of debtors and creditors, and in the public interest in reasonable and adequate information to evaluate the efficiency and practicality of the Federal bankruptcy system. In issuing rules proposing the forms referred to in subsection (a), the Attorney General shall strike the best achievable practical balance between—

    (1) the reasonable needs of the public for information about the operational results of the Federal bankruptcy system;

    (2) economy, simplicity, and lack of undue burden on persons with a duty to file reports; and

    (3) appropriate privacy concerns and safeguards.

(d) Final Reports.—The uniform forms for final reports required under subsection (a) for use by trustees under chapters 7, 12, and 13 of title 11shall, in addition to such other matters as are required by law or as the Attorney General in the discretion of the Attorney General shall propose, include with respect to a case under such title—

(1) information about the length of time the case was pending;

(2) assets abandoned;

(3) assets exempted;

(4) receipts and disbursements of the estate;

(5) expenses of administration, including for use under section 707(b), actual costs of administering cases under chapter 13 of title 11;

(6) claims asserted;

(7) claims allowed; and

(8) distributions to claimants and claims discharged without payment, in each case by appropriate category and, in cases under chapters 12 and 13 of title 11, date of confirmation of the plan, each modification thereto, and defaults by the debtor in performance under the plan.

(e) Periodic Reports.—The uniform forms for periodic reports required under subsection (a) for use by trustees or debtors in possession under chapter 11 of title 11 shall, in addition to such other matters as are required by law or as the Attorney General in the discretion of the Attorney General shall propose, include—

(1) information about the industry classification, published by the Department of Commerce, for the businesses conducted by the debtor;

(2) length of time the case has been pending;

(3) number of full-time employees as of the date of the order for relief and at the end of each reporting period since the case was filed;

(4) cash receipts, cash disbursements and profitability of the debtor for the most recent period and cumulatively since the date of the order for relief;

(5) compliance with title 11, whether or not tax returns and tax payments since the date of the order for relief have been timely filed and made;

(6) all professional fees approved by the court in the case for the most recent period and cumulatively since the date of the order for relief (separately reported, for the professional fees incurred by or on behalf of the debtor, between those that would have been incurred absent a bankruptcy case and those not); and

(7) plans of reorganization filed and confirmed and, with respect thereto, by class, the recoveries of the holders, expressed in aggregate dollar values and, in the case of claims, as a percentage of total claims of the class allowed.

Chapter 57 – General Provisions Applicable to Court Officers and Employees (Excerpt)

§959 - Trustees and receivers suable; management; State laws

(a) Trustees, receivers or managers of any property, including debtors in possession, may be sued, without leave of the court appointing them, with respect to any of their acts or transactions in carrying on business connected with such property. Such actions shall be subject to the general equity power of such court so far as the same may be necessary to the ends of justice, but this shall not deprive a litigant of his right to trial by jury.

(b) Except as provided in section 1166 of title 11, a trustee, receiver or manager appointed in any cause pending in any court of the United States, including a debtor in possession, shall manage and operate the property in his possession as such trustee, receiver or manager according to the requirements of the valid laws of the State in which such property is situated, in the same manner that the owner or possessor thereof would be bound to do if in possession thereof.

Chapter 85 – District Courts; Jurisdiction (Excerpt)

§1334. Bankruptcy cases and proceedings

(a) Except as provided in subsection (b) of this section, the district courts shall have original and exclusive jurisdiction of all cases under title 11.

(b) Except as provided in subsection (e)(2), and notwithstanding any Act of Congress that confers exclusive jurisdiction on a court or courts other than the district courts, the district courts shall have original but not exclusive jurisdiction of all civil proceedings arising under title 11, or arising in or related to cases under title 11.

(c)

    (1) Except with respect to a case under chapter 15 of title 11, nothing in this section prevents a district court in the interest of justice, or in the interest of comity with State courts or respect for State law, from abstaining from hearing a particular proceeding arising under title 11 or arising in or related to a case under title 11.

    (2) Upon timely motion of a party in a proceeding based upon a State law claim or State law cause of action, related to a case under title 11 but not arising under title 11 or arising in a case under title 11, with respect to which an action could not have been commenced in a court of the United States absent jurisdiction under this section, the district court shall abstain from hearing such proceeding if an action is commenced, and can be timely adjudicated, in a State forum of appropriate jurisdiction.

(d) Any decision to abstain or not to abstain made under subsection (c) (other than a decision not to abstain in a proceeding described in subsection (c)(2)) is not reviewable by appeal or otherwise by the court of appeals under section 158(d), 1291, or 1292 of this title or by the Supreme Court of the United States under section 1254 of this title. Subsection (c) and this subsection shall not be construed to limit the applicability of the stay provided for by section 362 of title 11, United States Code, as such section applies to an action affecting the property of the estate in bankruptcy.

(e) The district court in which a case under title 11 is commenced or is pending shall have exclusive jurisdiction—

    (1) of all the property, wherever located, of the debtor as of the commencement of such case, and of property of the estate; and

    (2) over all claims or causes of action that involve construction of section 327 of title 11, United States Code, or rules relating to disclosure requirements under section 327.

Chapter 87 – District Courts; Venue (Excerpt)

§1408 - Venue of cases under title 11

Except as provided in section 1410 of this title, a case under title 11 may be commenced in the district court for the district—

    (1) in which the domicile, residence, principal place of business in the United States, or principal assets in the United States, of the person or entity that is the subject of such case have been located for the one hundred and eighty days immediately preceding such commencement, or for a longer portion of such one-hundred-and-eighty-day period than the domicile, residence, or principal place of business, in the United States, or principal assets in the United States, of such person were located in any other district; or

    (2) in which there is pending a case under title 11 concerning such person's affiliate, general partner, or partnership.

§1409 - Venue of proceedings arising under title 11 or arising in or related to cases under title 11

(a) Except as otherwise provided in subsections (b) and (d), a proceeding arising under title 11 or arising in or related to a case under title 11 may be commenced in the district court in which such case is pending.

(b) Except as provided in subsection (d) of this section, a trustee in a case under title 11 may commence a proceeding arising in or related to such case to recover a money judgment of or property worth less than $1,000 or a consumer debt of less than $15,000, or a debt (excluding a consumer debt) against a noninsider of less than $10,000, only in the district court for the district in which the defendant resides.

(c) Except as provided in subsection (b) of this section, a trustee in a case under title 11 may commence a proceeding arising in or related to such case as statutory successor to the debtor or creditors under section 541 or 544(b) of title 11in the district court for the district where the State or Federal court sits in which, under applicable nonbankruptcy venue provisions, the debtor or creditors, as the case may be, may have commenced an action on which such proceeding is based if the case under title 11 had not been commenced.

(d) A trustee may commence a proceeding arising under title 11 or arising in or related to a case under title 11 based on a claim arising after the commencement of such case from the operation of the business of the debtor only in the district court for the district where a State or Federal court sits in which, under applicable nonbankruptcy venue provisions, an action on such claim may have been brought.

(e) A proceeding arising under title 11 or arising in or related to a case under title 11, based on a claim arising after the commencement of such case from the operation of the business of the debtor, may be commenced against the representative of the estate in such case in the district court for the district where the State or Federal court sits in which the party commencing such proceeding may, under applicable nonbankruptcy venue provisions, have brought an action on such claim, or in the district court in which such case is pending.

§1410 - Venue of cases ancillary to foreign proceedings

A case under chapter 15 of title 11 may be commenced in the district court of the United States for the district—

(1) in which the debtor has its principal place of business or principal assets in the United States;

(2) if the debtor does not have a place of business or assets in the United States, in which there is pending against the debtor an action or proceeding in a Federal or State court; or

(3) in a case other than those specified in paragraph (1) or (2), in which venue will be consistent with the interests of justice and the convenience of the parties, having regard to the relief sought by the foreign representative.

§1411 - Jury trials

(a) Except as provided in subsection (b) of this section, this chapter and title 11 do not affect any right to trial by jury that an individual has under applicable nonbankruptcy law with regard to a personal injury or wrongful death tort claim.

(b) The district court may order the issues arising under section 303 of title 11 to be tried without a jury.

§1412 - Change of venue

A district court may transfer a case or proceeding under title 11 to a district court for another district, in the interest of justice or for the convenience of the parties.

Chapter 89 – District Courts; Removal of Cases from State Courts (Excerpt)

§1452 - Removal of claims related to bankruptcy cases

(a) A party may remove any claim or cause of action in a civil action other than a proceeding before the United States Tax Court or a civil action by a governmental unit to enforce such governmental unit's police or regulatory power, to the district court for the district where such civil action is pending, if such district court has jurisdiction of such claim or cause of action under section 1334 of this title.

(b) The court to which such claim or cause of action is removed may remand such claim or cause of action on any equitable ground. An order entered under this subsection remanding a claim or cause of action, or a decision to not remand, is not reviewable by appeal or otherwise by the court of appeals under section 158(d), 1291, or 1292 of this title or by the Supreme Court of the United States under section 1254 of this title.

Chapter 111 – General Provisions (Excerpt)

§1655 - Lien enforcement; absent defendants

In an action in a district court to enforce any lien upon or claim to, or to remove any incumbrance or lien or cloud upon the title to, real or personal property within the district, where any defendant cannot be served within the State, or does not voluntarily appear, the court may order the absent defendant to appear or plead by a day certain.

Such order shall be served on the absent defendant personally if practicable, wherever found, and also upon the person or persons in possession or charge of such property, if any. Where personal service is not practicable, the order shall be published as the court may direct, not less than once a week for six consecutive weeks.

If an absent defendant does not appear or plead within the time allowed, the court may proceed as if the absent defendant had been served with process within the State, but any adjudication shall, as regards the absent defendant without appearance, affect only the property which is the subject of the action.

When a part of the property is within another district, but within the same state, such action may be brought in either district.

Any defendant not so personally notified may, at any time within one year after final judgment, enter his appearance, and thereupon the court shall set aside the judgment and permit such defendant to plead on payment of such costs as the court deems just.

Chapter 123 – Fees and Costs (Excerpt)

§1930 - Bankruptcy fees

(a) The parties commencing a case under title 11 shall pay to the clerk of the district court or the clerk of the bankruptcy court, if one has been certified pursuant to section 156(b) of this title, the following filing fees:

(1) For a case commenced under—

(A) chapter 7 of title 11, $245, and

(B) chapter 13 of title 11, $235.

(2) For a case commenced under chapter 9 of title 11, equal to the fee specified in paragraph (3) for filing a case under chapter 11 of title 11. The amount by which the fee payable under this paragraph exceeds $300 shall be deposited in the fund established under section 1931 of this title.

(3) For a case commenced under chapter 11 of title 11 that does not concern a railroad, as defined in section 101 of title 11, $1,167.

(4) For a case commenced under chapter 11 of title 11 concerning a railroad, as so defined, $1,000.

(5) For a case commenced under chapter 12 of title 11, $200.

(6) In addition to the filing fee paid to the clerk, a quarterly fee shall be paid to the United States trustee, for deposit in the Treasury, in each case under chapter 11 of title 11 for each quarter (including any fraction thereof) until the case is converted or dismissed, whichever occurs first. The fee shall be $325 for each quarter in which disbursements total less than $15,000; $650 for each quarter in which disbursements total $15,000 or more but less than $75,000; $975 for each quarter in which disbursements total $75,000 or more but less than $150,000; $1,625 for each quarter in which disbursements total $150,000 or more but less than $225,000; $1,950 for each quarter in which disbursements total $225,000 or more but less than $300,000; $4,875 for each quarter in which disbursements total $300,000 or more but less than $1,000,000; $6,500 for each quarter in which disbursements total $1,000,000 or more but less than $2,000,000; $9,750 for each quarter in which disbursements total $2,000,000 or more but less than $3,000,000; $10,400 for each quarter in which

disbursements total $3,000,000 or more but less than $5,000,000; $13,000 for each quarter in which disbursements total $5,000,000 or more but less than $15,000,000; $20,000 for each quarter in which disbursements total $15,000,000 or more but less than $30,000,000; $30,000 for each quarter in which disbursements total more than $30,000,000. The fee shall be payable on the last day of the calendar month following the calendar quarter for which the fee is owed.

(7) In districts that are not part of a United States trustee region as defined in section 581 of this title, the Judicial Conference of the United States may require the debtor in a case under chapter 11 of title 11 to pay fees equal to those imposed by paragraph (6) of this subsection. Such fees shall be deposited as offsetting receipts to the fund established under section 1931 of this title and shall remain available until expended.

An individual commencing a voluntary case or a joint case under title 11 may pay such fee in installments. For converting, on request of the debtor, a case under chapter 7, or 13 of title 11, to a case under chapter 11 of title 11, the debtor shall pay to the clerk of the district court or the clerk of the bankruptcy court, if one has been certified pursuant to section 156(b) of this title, a fee of the amount equal to the difference between the fee specified in paragraph (3) and the fee specified in paragraph (1).

(b) The Judicial Conference of the United States may prescribe additional fees in cases under title 11 of the same kind as the Judicial Conference prescribes under section 1914(b) of this title.

(c) Upon the filing of any separate or joint notice of appeal or application for appeal or upon the receipt of any order allowing, or notice of the allowance of, an appeal or a writ of certiorari $5 shall be paid to the clerk of the court, by the appellant or petitioner.

(d) Whenever any case or proceeding is dismissed in any bankruptcy court for want of jurisdiction, such court may order the payment of just costs.

(e) The clerk of the court may collect only the fees prescribed under this section.

(f)

(1) Under the procedures prescribed by the Judicial Conference of the United States, the district court or the bankruptcy court may waive the filing fee in a case under chapter 7 of title 11 for an individual if the court determines that such individual has income less than 150 percent of the income official poverty line (as defined by the Office of Management and Budget, and revised annually in accordance with section 673(2) of the Omnibus Budget Reconciliation Act of 1981) applicable to a family of the size involved and is unable to pay that fee in installments. For purposes of this paragraph, the term "filing fee" means the filing fee required by subsection (a), or any other fee

prescribed by the Judicial Conference under subsections (b) and (c) that is payable to the clerk upon the commencement of a case under chapter 7.

(2) The district court or the bankruptcy court may waive for such debtors other fees prescribed under subsections (b) and (c).

(3) This subsection does not restrict the district court or the bankruptcy court from waiving, in accordance with Judicial Conference policy, fees prescribed under this section for other debtors and creditors.

Chapter 131 – Rules of Courts (Excerpt)

§2075 - Bankruptcy rules

The Supreme Court shall have the power to prescribe by general rules, the forms of process, writs, pleadings, and motions, and the practice and procedure in cases under title 11.

Such rules shall not abridge, enlarge, or modify any substantive right.

The Supreme Court shall transmit to Congress not later than May 1 of the year in which a rule prescribed under this section is to become effective a copy of the proposed rule. The rule shall take effect no earlier than December 1 of the year in which it is transmitted to Congress unless otherwise provided by law.

The bankruptcy rules promulgated under this section shall prescribe a form for the statement required under section 707(b)(2)(C) of title 11 and may provide general rules on the content of such statement.